GOT QUESTIONS?

Got Answers

VOLUME ONE

Common Questions Asked
by Christians and Religious
People Every Day

Rich Kanyali

Table of Contents

Acknowledgments and Special Thanks

I would like to give special thanks to the following people who have made and continue to make a major positive impact on my life:

Jesus Christ–Lord, You are my personal Lord and Savior. You have been my Guide and Teacher. Lord, I thank You for changing my life and blessing me beyond measure. I adore You and I'm forever grateful for Your finished work on the cross. Thank You so much for Your unconditional and infinite love for me. Thank You for increased and supernatural revelation You have given me through Your Word and the anointing to communicate it with simplicity and clarity. I trust and totally depend on You. Thank you for the lives you are going to speak to and touch through this book. I give You all the glory and honor, the Lover of my soul. Thank You, Lord Jesus.

Andrew Wommack (President and Founder–Andrew Wommack Ministries and Charis Bible College)–It's an absolute privilege and an honor to serve at your ministry. I have learned a lot from you over the past many years. You have taught and inspired me so much. Your humility is very admirable. Things I have learned from you have guided and transformed my life and have birthed many books that I have written and will write. Thank you, so very much.

Pastor Greg Mohr (Director of Charis Bible College)–Pastor Greg, you are a man of wisdom and humility. You have taught me so much. Thank you for pouring out your heart to help grow, change, and impact my life. I'm forever grateful.

Pastor Rick McFarland (Dean of Education, Charis Bible College)–Pastor Rick, you are my pastor and mentor. I look up to you and I greatly appreciate all you and your wife (Pastor Joann McFarland) have invested in me and spoken into my life. I continue to learn and grow through your mentorship and guidance. Thank you very much.

Mr. Barry Bennett (Dean of Instructors, Charis bible College)–Mr. Barry, It has been humbling to know you and to learn from your teachings. Many things I have learned from you. Thank you so much. Your teachings have transformed my life. Thank you, sir.

Thank you all for impacting and changing my life.

Introduction

I have had the heart to help answer people's questions since childhood, and I still do today. When I first got born again, I had so many questions that the Lord answered over the years. This desire to answer questions later led me to Charis Bible college for ministry training, where I graduated with a Master's in Biblical Studies and now serve as the Assistant Dean of Education. However, I have come to realize that not all questions have the same motive of knowing the truth. Some questions are to debate, cast doubt, or argue. We must learn to discern the spirit behind the question. Some questions have a preconceived notion, while others are accusatory, others are assumptive, and other questions may only be a trap. Not all questions are created equal, nor in the same image. Therefore, not all questions need to be answered.

> "But foolish and unlearned questions avoid, knowing that they do gender strifes."
>
> – 2 Timothy 2:23

I must confess that none of us have all the answers. That's why we need to learn to walk by faith. The Word of God clearly teaches that, in this life, we know in part (1 Corinthians 13:12). Yet, I believe that *part* that we do know is big enough for us to live a victorious Christian life. For all the answers that we genuinely need to know, the Lord has already provided in God's Word.

Do not throw away what you do know because of what you do not know.

I will be shooting straight in the attempt to answer these questions as quickly and directly as possible. My approach will be mostly in a teaching format or style. This way I can answer the question, and at the same time also impart some guidance, teaching, reproof, and instruction to build you up. I believe in the infallibility of the Word of God; therefore, all my answers will be derived from the Holy Bible and the revelation that God has given me—some directly and some through other people. I believe there is no better source of answers than the Word of God, therefore, I will stick with what the Word of God teaches. Asking and answering questions are a huge foundation for learning to the one asking and the one being asked.

Buckle up, and let's roll.

Chapter One

Is the Bible the Word of God?

"Down through the years it's been ridiculed, burned, refuted, destroyed, but it lives on. It is the anvil that has worn out many hammers. Most books are born, live a few short years, then go the way of all the earth; they're forgotten. But not the Bible." –Billy Graham.

This question is not a new question. It has been around and will continue to be. Many people try to challenge and dispute the integrity of God's Word, but a close study of the Bible confirms clearly how it is the Word of God. Among all books in the world, the Bible has suffered the most, been persecuted the most, and above all, it is the only book that has been sought to be destroyed by most governments. Why? Because of the power and truth contained within its pages.

In order to have a vibrant relationship with the Lord, we must have complete trust and faith in His Word. We can't have a vibrant relationship with the Lord outside of His Word. **Our relationship with God's Word is directly equivalent to our relationship with Him.**

The Bible was written by 40 writers, over a period of 1,600 years, in 66 books. And the great theme from one end of the Bible to the other is redemption–God's love for mankind, and God redeeming and bringing man back to Himself after man fell because of sin. That's what the Bible is all about.

It is the **world's best-seller of all time** and the only book that has been translated into nearly all languages. Yet this book, for the past 200 years, has been under increased attack. Many people, even within the church, have come to doubt whether the Bible is authoritative and trustworthy. If we do not believe in the Bible, how can we believe in Jesus, since the only knowledge we have of Jesus Christ is in the Bible? Throughout the rest of this chapter, I'll show you the overwhelming evidence of why we can trust the Bible.

One thing that may lead a person to doubt if the Bible is God's Word is the knowledge that it was written by man. Some people can't wrap their mind around the fact that God used man to write His Word. Little do they know or have considered, that the way God works here on earth is through people, even though this truth has its fingerprints in pretty much all affairs of man. If God wants to give you kids, He will give you a spouse. That's also working through people (man). Furthermore, for God to save the world from sin, He had to become man. An understanding of this makes it even simpler to believe that the Bible is the Word of God although written by and through man.

Man was the **writer** that God chose to use, but the Holy Spirit (God) was the very **author** of the Bible. There is a big difference between a **writer** and an **author. God is the Author of the Bible, not man. Man is just the writer.**

A. All Scripture is inspired of God

> *"All scripture is given by inspiration of God, and is profitable for doctrine, for reproof, for correction, for instruction in righteousness: That the man of God may be perfect, thoroughly furnished unto all good works."*
> —2 Timothy 3:16-17

a) This verse clearly says that **ALL** scripture is given by inspiration of God. The Greek word for "inspiration" means "divinely breathed" (Strong's Concordance). In other words, man was inspired and moved by God to write. The Bible is not full of knowledge and wisdom from man, but from God. In other words, God the Holy Spirit dictated and guided a few chosen people to write His Word.

b) All Scripture is given by inspiration of God, NOT given by inspiration of man.

c) The Amplified Version says, "All Scripture is **God-breathed** [given by divine inspiration] and is profitable for instruction, for conviction [of sin], for correction [of error and restoration to obedience], for training in righteousness [learning to live in conformity to God's will, both publicly and privately–behaving honorably with personal integrity and moral courage];"

    i) This translation uses the word "God-breathed" for the word "inspiration." In other words, the word *God-breathed* is synonymous to *God-inspired*.

    ii) The Bible is God's inspired and breathed Word.

B. Moved by the Holy Spirit

"Knowing this first, that no prophecy of the Scripture is of any private inter-pretation. For the prophecy came not in old time by the will of man: but holy men of God spake as they were moved by the Holy Ghost."

—2 Peter 1:20-21

This passage is simply saying that the scriptures are divinely inspired and were not the revelation of man, but God.

The Word of God including the Old Covenant is not opinions of men, but rather God. It is God-breathed. These men who were used by God to write the Word were not doing this according to their will or just expressing their way of thought, ideas, and mind. They were simply providing or expressing the heart and mind of God as they were led by Him to write.

God opened the mouth of a donkey–that was dumb and had no knowledge or understanding–to speak effectively and clearly to Balaam the prophet (Numbers 22:28-33). How much more can God move, speak, and effectively and accurately convey His message to all people through Holy men of God who are smarter than a donkey, have more understanding, and are created in His own image?

C. Jesus' faith in the Bible

This might come as a surprise to many, but **Jesus quoted the Bible**. I have to point out that if He had no faith in the Bible, He would have never quoted it. If He had no faith in it, He would not have referenced it repeatedly. He repeatedly quoted the prophets and the Old Testament, which shows His faith and trust in the Bible and its authenticity. Before we reject, disregard or even dispute the Bible, this is quite a point to consider. Jesus had faith in the Bible, and He quoted it.

Below is a table I have compiled that will show you how Jesus quoted the Word of God in the Old Testament, hence showing faith in its authenticity and infallibility.

New Testament Quote of Old Testament Scripture	Old Testament Scripture
Jesus references Psalms when foretelling Jerusalem's destruction (Matthew 23:39; Luke 13:35).	Psalm 118:26
He quotes Psalms to the chief priests and elders, calling Himself the chief cornerstone (Matthew 21:42; Mark 12:10; Luke 20:17).	Psalm 118:22–23
Jesus quotes Psalm 110 when Pilate asks if He is the son of God (Matthew 26:64).	Psalm 118:22–23
When the Jews want to stone Jesus for claiming to be God, He responds with a verse in Psalms (John 10:34).	Psalm 82:6
Jesus recalls the manna in the wilderness after feeding a multitude (John 6:31).	Psalm 78:24

He quotes the Psalms when talking about His betrayal (John 13:18).	Psalm 41:9
Jesus is hated without cause, which He says the Psalms foretold (John 15:25).	Psalm 35:19; 69:4
He quotes the twenty-second Psalm while dying on the cross: "My God, my God, why have you forsaken me?" (Matthew 27:46; Mark 15:34). He then fulfills the thirty-first Psalm by committing His spirit to the Father (Luke 23:46).	Psalm 22:1; 31:5
Jesus outwits the Pharisees with the Psalms on several occasions (Matthew 21:16, 22:44; Mark 12:36, 14:62; Luke 20:42–43).	Psalm 8:2 110:1
When Satan tempts Jesus in the wilderness, Jesus responds with passages from Deuteronomy (Matthew 4:4, 7, 10; Luke 4:4, 8, 12).	Deuteronomy 6:13, 16, 8:3
He mentions Moses' rule of witnesses when He outlines church discipline (Matthew 18:16).	Deuteronomy 19:15
Jesus references Deuteronomy when He discusses divorce (Matthew 5:31, 19:7; Mark 10:4).	Deuteronomy 24:1–3
Jesus sums up the law and the prophets with a line from Deuteronomy (and another from Leviticus): love God and love your neighbor as yourself (Matthew 22:37; Mark 12:29–33; Luke 10:27).	Deuteronomy 6:5
He heals the blind and brings good news to the afflicted (Matthew 11:5; Luke 4:18–19, 7:22).	Isaiah 61:1–2
His salvation ministry allows the people to be taught of God (John 6:45).	Isaiah 54:13
He quotes Isaiah's prophecy that Jesus would die a sinner's death (Luke 22:37).	Isaiah 53:12

He alludes to Isaiah in His parable of the vineyard (Matthew 21:33; Mark 12:1; Luke 20:9).	Isaiah 5:1
He calls out the Pharisees and scribes for their lip service to God—they honor God with their words, but their hearts are far from him (Matthew 15:8–9; Mark 7:6–7).	Isaiah 29:13
When Jesus turns over the tables in the temple, He references Isaiah's words on how the house of God was intended to operate (Matthew 21:13; Mark 11:17; Luke 19:46).	Isaiah 56:7
Jesus speaks in parables, fulfilling Isaiah's prophecy concerning "eyes that do not see" and "ears that do not hear" (Matthew 13:14–15; Mark 4:12; Luke 8:10).	Isaiah 6:9–10
Jesus quotes the famous "eye for an eye" line right before telling His disciples to turn the other cheek (Matthew 5:38).	Exodus 21:24
And of course, the commandments against murder and adultery show up in Jesus' Sermon on the Mount (Matthew 5:21, 27).	Exodus 20:12–13
He mentions the fifth commandment (honoring parents) when exposing the Pharisees' and scribes' hypocrisy (Matthew 15:4; Mark 7:10).	Exodus 20:12, 21:17
He recalls the Ten Commandments when telling a rich man how to enter the kingdom of God (Matthew 19:18–19; Mark 10:19; Luke 18:20).	Exodus 20:12–16
Jesus references the burning bush incident when explaining the resurrection (Matthew 22:32; Mark 12:26; Luke 20:37).	Exodus 3:6

D. God has revealed Himself to us through His Word (the Bible).

"And the LORD appeared again in Shiloh: for the LORD revealed himself to Samuel in Shiloh by the word of the LORD."

–1 Samuel 3:21

a) The Word is what reveals God and Jesus to us. Without the Bible–God's written inspired Word–we couldn't know Jesus. The way God revealed Himself to Samuel, was by His Word. The Bible is the Word of God through which He reveals Himself to us. If it weren't His Word, He wouldn't have revealed Himself through it.

E. God has magnified His Word above His Name.

"I will worship toward thy holy temple, and praise thy name for thy loving-kindness and for thy truth: for thou hast magnified thy word above all thy name."

–Psalm 138:2

a) **For thou hast magnified thy word above all thy name**

   i) Nothing is greater, or no name is greater, than the name of Jesus; BUT God has exalted His Word even above His name. God's Word is so powerful that it is magnified above His name.

   ii) If the Bible (God's written Word) was not God's Word, He would not have exalted it above His name that is above all names.

b) Luke 4:32, *"And they were astonished at his doctrine: for his **word** was with power"* (emphasis mine).

   i) God's Word, both spoken and written is full of power.

F. Scientific accuracy

a) *"He stretcheth out the north over the empty place, and hangeth the earth upon nothing."* –Job 26:7

i) This verse clearly teaches that the earth hangs upon nothing, yet the scientists of Job's day didn't know this. How did Job know that the earth hung in space (upon nothing) before the age of modern astronomy and space travel? God revealed this to him through His Word. This was way back between 1650 BC and 1500 BC during the lifetime of Job.

ii) The scientists of our days have just figured this out not very long ago. If they were in tune with the Word of God, they would have known this since Job spoke about it long ago.

b) *"For the life of the flesh is in the blood: and I have given it to you upon the altar to make an atonement for your souls: for it is the blood that maketh an atonement for the soul."* –Leviticus 17:11

i) George Washington's experience is one example of how the life of the flesh is in the blood. He died as a result of being bled out (bloodletting). He asked to have his overseer George Rawlins come to bleed him. Washington was bled by Rawlins and later by doctors four times over the course of the next eight hours. Today doctors estimate half of his blood was drained. He later died in that same year of 1799. At this time in history, it was believed that by draining out the blood they would receive healing, yet they died even quicker.

ii) Had Washington's doctor known what is said in Leviticus 17:11 that "the life of the flesh is in the blood," had the scientists and physicians of George Washington's day known what the Bible taught; many lives could have been saved including George Washington's.

iii) This is perfect evidence that the Word of God is true. During Washington's day doctors did not understand that the life of the flesh is in the blood. Yet, this biological fact is clearly stated in the Book of Leviticus thousands of years earlier. How could Moses, the writer of Leviticus, have known this? Moses knew this because Scripture is God-breathed.

c) *"It is he that sitteth upon the circle of the earth, and the inhabitants thereof are as grasshoppers; that stretcheth out the heavens as a curtain, and spreadeth them out as a tent to dwell in."* –Isaiah 40:22

   i) The word for "circle" here means a globe or sphere. How did Isaiah know that God sits upon the circle of the earth? By divine inspiration.

   ii) The scientists of Isaiah's day didn't know the configuration of the surface of the earth, yet Isaiah included this fact.

   iii) Isaiah was way ahead of all the scientists of his day because he spoke of the earth being of circle shape before scientists ever figured this out. God revealed to him that the earth was a sphere shape.

G. The Law of the Lord is perfect.

"The law of the LORD is perfect, converting the soul: the testimony of the LORD is sure, making wise the simple. The statutes of the LORD are right, rejoicing the heart: the commandment of the LORD is pure, enlightening the eyes. The fear of the LORD is clean, enduring forever: the judgments of the LORD are true and righteous altogether. More to be desired are they than gold, yea, than much fine gold: sweeter also than honey and the honeycomb."

–Psalm 19:7-10

a) **The Law of the Lord is perfect.**

   i) This means the "statute or precept", in other words, the Word of God.

   ii) The Hebrew word from which "Perfect" is translated means "entire; also (as noun) integrity, truth."

   • It is without blemish; it is complete, full, sincere, sound, undefiled, and upright.

b) **Converting the soul**

   i) "Converting" means to turn back.

   ii) "Soul" means a "breathing creature".

- The Word of God has the power to change any breathing creature. His Word is complete, entire, without spot, without blemish, sound and undefiled. Nothing else has the power to turn back a soul but God's Word.

c) **The testimony of the LORD *is* sure.**

   i) The "law of the Lord" is used interchangeably with the "testimony of the Lord". So, the law of the Lord = the testimony of the Lord.

- The Word of the Lord is the witness of the Lord.
- The word "sure" used in this verse means "firm." We can build our lives on the Word of God because it is firm. It should be trusted to support our lives.
- "Sure" simply means "to be true." God's Word is for real. It's for sure.

d) **The statutes of the LORD *are* right.**

   i) We live in a time in which people debate and doubt if the written Word of God (The Bible) is right. This verse should settle that argument. The Word of God is right. If you think or do things contrary to the Holy Word of God, you are wrong. It doesn't matter what you feel or what your professor says, God's Word is right.

   ii) Another way of saying this is that the Word of God (The Bible) is correct, straight and upright.

e) **The commandment of the LORD is pure.**

   i) God's Word is void of any contamination. It is unpolluted. It is unadulterated. It is clear, clean, and sincere.

ii) Although many people in our societies say that God's Word is corrupted and altered, we know that is simply not the case. God's Word is pure. It has not been adulterated, and it is neither corrupted nor contaminated. Anyone who says otherwise is in error because God's Word is right. God cannot lie. If He says His Word is right, I believe Him.

H. The Word of the LORD is right

"For the word of the LORD is right; and all his works are done in truth."

–Psalm 33:4

a) The Hebrew word translated for "right" means "straight".

i) God's Word is not bent in any way. It's straight and accurate. It's right. It ought to be the direction and standard of everything we do because it is right and never fails.

b) **Two scriptures that speak to the accuracy of God's Word are Isaiah 55:11 and Psalm 33:9.**

i) "So shall my word be that goeth forth out of my mouth: it shall not return unto me void, but it shall accomplish that which I please, and it shall prosper in the thing whereto I sent it." –Isaiah 55:11. Since God's Word is accurate, it will fulfill that which it promises to do.

ii) "He spoke, and it was done, and He commanded, and it stood fast." –Psalm 33:9

I. God's Word is truth.

"Sanctify them through thy truth: thy word is truth."

–John 17:17

a) Thy Word is truth.

i) God's Word = Truth. Not God's Word = not truth.

ii) The word "Truth" is defined as below:

- Conformity to fact or reality
- The true state of facts or things
- Conformity of words to thoughts, which is called moral truth
- Correct opinion, Fidelity; constancy; honesty; virtue; sincerity

J. God's Word never fails.

"For as the rain cometh down, and the snow from heaven, and returneth not thither, but watereth the earth, and maketh it bring forth and bud, that it may give seed to the sower, and bread to the eater: So shall my word be that goeth forth out of my mouth: it shall not return unto me void, but it shall accomplish that which I please, and it shall prosper in the thing whereto I sent it."

–Isaiah 55:10-11

a) God's Word never fails. He says, and it is established. He compared it to how rain and snow come down from heaven and does not return there but waters the ground.

   i) God's Word is infallible. This is what this is saying. It's a seed that will grow and bring forth fruit.

   ii) It accomplishes what God desires and pleases. God's Word does not accomplish anything but that which is only according to God's will, heart, and desire.

   iii) It shall prosper. God's Word will not fail. It will prosper and excel in what it's directed to do. It always prospers and produces results.

K. Born again through the Word

"Being born again, not of corruptible seed, but of incorruptible, by the Word of God, which liveth and abideth forever."

–1 Peter 1:23

We are born again (saved) through the Word of God. The Bible is the written Word of God. Without it, we can't be saved because it reveals the Lord to us and how we can be saved. The Word of God is the complete revelation of who God is.

a) God's Word is a SEED. An incorruptible seed. It cannot be corrupted.

b) We are born again by this incorruptible seed which is the Word of God.

c) Faith comes by hearing and hearing by the Word of God (Romans 10:10-17).

   i) Therefore, we must preach and sow this incorruptible seed, the Word of God, so that salvation can occur. No Word (SEED), no salvation (born again).

d) If the Bible is not God's written Word and is not accurate and truthful like some have suggested, then we cannot be born again. We are lost because the very seed for our salvation to occur is not reliable. Jesus would have to come again.

L. Fulfilled Prophecy

Did you know the Bible is the only book in the world that has accurate prophecy? When you read the prophecies of the Bible and see how they were supernaturally fulfilled, you simply have to stand back in wonder. There are over 300 precise prophecies that deal with the Lord Jesus Christ in the Old Testament that are fulfilled in the New Testament. To say that these are fulfilled by chance is an astronomical impossibility. It is nonsensical.

Old Testament prophecy fulfillment is one of the greatest arguments for the Bible being God's Word. **This is one of the most convincing arguments that the Bible is true.** It's important to note that all these prophecies were given thousands and hundreds of years before, yet they were fulfilled perfectly.

In Acts Chapter Two, as Peter preached to the people under the inspiration of the Holy Ghost, he quoted Old Testament scriptures to prove to them that

Jesus was indeed the Messiah. To someone sincerely seeking the truth, this is an irresistible argument.

The way these scriptural prophecies played out, no one can argue with the truth that the Bible is true indeed. The fulfillment of these scriptures cannot be a coincidence.

Here are some of the Old Testament prophecies and their New Testament fulfillment:

OLD TESTAMENT REFERENCE	PROPHECY	NEW TESTAMENT FULFILLMENT
Genesis 3:15	Victory over Satan	Colossians 2:15
Numbers 21:9	Type of serpent	John 3:14-15
Psalm 16: 10	The Messiah would not see corruption	Acts 2:27, 31; 13:35
Psalm 22:1	Christ forsaken	Matthew 27:46; Mark 15:34
Psalm 22:7-8	Messiah mocked and ridiculed	Luke 23:35
Psalm 22:16	Piercing of His hands and feet	Mark 15:25; Luke 23:33; John 19:37; 20:25
Psalm 22:18	Parting His garments and casting lots for them	Luke 23:34; John 19:23-24
Psalm 34:20	Not one bone broken	John 19:36
Psalm 35:11	Accused falsely	Mark 14:57-58
Psalm 35:19	Hated without a cause	John 15:24-25
Psalm 41:9	Betrayed by a close associate	Luke 22:47-48
Psalm 49:15	His resurrection	Mark 16:6-7
Psalm 68:18	His ascension to God's right hand	Mark 16:19; Ephesians 4:8
Psalm 69:21	Given vinegar to drink in His thirst	Matthew 27:34, 48; Mark 15:36; John 19:29

Psalm 109:25	They reviled Him, wagging their heads	Matthew 27:39
Isaiah 50:6	They spit in His face	Matthew 26:67
Isaiah 50:6	The Messiah scourged	Matthew 27:26
Isaiah 52:14	Lost human appearance by physical mistreatment	Matthew 27:26; Mark 15:15
Isaiah 52:15	Gentiles shall receive spiritual cleansing	Hebrews 1:3
Isaiah 53:3	He was despised and rejected of men	John 1:10-11
Isaiah 53:4	He bore our sickness	Matthew 8:16-17
Isaiah 53:5-6	He was wounded for our transgressions	Romans 4:25; 1 Peter 3:1
Isaiah 53:7	He opened not His mouth	Matthew 26:63; 27:12, 14; Mark 15:5; 1 Peter 2:235
Isaiah 53:9	He was buried with the rich	Matthew 27:57-58, 60
Isaiah 53:11	He shall justify many	Romans 3:26, 5:19
Isaiah 53:12	He was numbered with the transgressors	Mark 15:28; Luke 22:37
Isaiah 53:12	He was crucified with criminals	Mark 15:27-28
Jonah 1:17	The sign of the prophet Jonah	Matthew 12:40; 16:4
Micah 5:1	Smitten with the rod upon the cheek	Matthew 27:30
Zechariah 11:12	He was betrayed for thirty pieces of silver	Matthew 26:15
Zechariah 11:13	The betrayal money was used to buy the potter's field	Matthew 26:15
Zechariah 13:7	The shepherd is smitten, and the flock is scattered	Matthew 26:31; Mark 14:27

Compiled and edited as cited in **Christian Philosophy** by Andrew Wommack

The Bible in American History

To wrap up this chapter, which I believe proves that the Bible is true and trustworthy, let's take a quick look at how the Bible is the foundation for the United States.

"I have examined all religions, and the result is that the Bible is the best book in the world."

–John Adams

"Suppose a nation in some distant region should take the Bible for their only law book and every member should regulate his conduct by the precepts there exhibited…What a Utopia – what a Paradise would this region be!"

–John Adams
(Signer of the declaration of independence; judge; diplomat;
one of two signers of the bill of rights; second president of United States)

Even though many do not know this, most societies are governed according to the principles of the Bible. Although we have strayed from it, most of, if not all government legal structure and system is derived and drawn primarily from biblical principles. Take for example the court and legal system, you need a witness to convict and sentence someone, just as the Bible tells us in Deuteronomy 19:15-21; 17. Another example is marriage, which was actually instituted by God, as well as justice, equality, and government (Romans 13).

"I verily believe Christianity necessary to the support of civil society. One of the beautiful boasts of our municipal jurisprudence is that Christianity is a part of the Common Law … There never has been a period in which the Common Law did not recognize Christianity as lying its foundations."

–Joseph Story
(Supreme Court Justice Joseph Story, Harvard Speech, 1829)

"Education is useless without the Bible. The Bible was America's basic textbook in all fields. God's Word, contained in the Bible, has furnished all necessary rules to direct our conduct."

–Noah Webster

I'm totally convinced that the Bible is God's Word. I pray this has helped you to believe God's Word and trust it (Isaiah 55:8-11).

Here is the bottom line of everything. No matter how many facts I can present to you to prove the infallibility of God's Word, you still retain the right to choose as you wish. You can choose to believe by faith that the Word is God's inerrant, incorruptible and infallible Word or not.

"[The Bible] is the rock on which our Republic rests."

–Andrew Jackson

Chapter Two

Why Does God Act Differently in the Old Testament than the New Testament?

Why Does God Deal With Mankind Before and After the Law, and Under Grace Differently?

Why did God Give the Law? What Was the Purpose of the Law?

One of the things we have to learn about God is that **He is a God of covenants**. He governs and He operates based on covenants. He deals with mankind based on covenants. The Old Covenant was one that God made with the children of Israel. It was a covenant that was based on the works and performance of the people of Israel. If they performed well, they were blessed and if they performed poorly, they were to be punished and cursed.

We see this in Deuteronomy 28 where it lists all the blessings and the curses. When the children of Israel entered into this covenant with God, they agreed to it in that, if they did well, they would be blessed and if they messed up, they would be cursed.

Let's look at these two verses from the Old Covenant

a) *"And all the people answered together, and said, All that the LORD hath spoken we will do. And Moses returned the words of the people unto the LORD."* –Exodus 19:8

b) *"And Moses came and told the people all the words of the LORD, and all the judgments: and all the people answered with one voice, and said, All the words which the LORD hath said will we do."* –Exodus 24:3

In other words, the children of Israel signed on the dotted line by saying we **agree (all that the Lord hath spoken we will do)**. So, if God was going to bless them when they did right, He was bound and obliged by the covenant to act by cursing and punishing them when they broke the law.

Coming to the New Covenant we have to first understand that this covenant is not the same as the Old Covenant. The Old Covenant is completely different from the New Testament. The New Covenant is explained in detail in the book of Hebrews:

a) *"But now hath he obtained a more excellent ministry, by how much also he is the mediator of a better covenant, which was established upon better promises. For if that first covenant had been faultless, then should no place have been sought for the second. For finding fault with them, he saith, Behold, the days come, saith the Lord, when I will make a new covenant with the house of Israel and with the house of Judah: Not according to the covenant that I made with their fathers in the day when I took them by the hand to lead them out of the land of Egypt; because they continued not in my covenant, and I regarded them not, saith the Lord. For this is the covenant that I will make with the house of Israel after those days, saith the Lord; I will put my laws into their mind, and write them in their hearts: and I will be to them a God, and they shall be to me a people: And they shall not teach every man his neighbor, and every man his brother, saying, Know the Lord: for all shall know me, from the least to the greatest. For I will be merciful to their unrighteousness, and their sins and their iniquities will I remember no more. In that he saith, A new covenant, he hath made the first old. Now that which decayeth and waxeth old is ready to vanish away."*–Hebrews 8:6-13

   i) The New Covenant is one that is established based on grace, not the people's performance. It was based on Jesus' obedience and sacrifice on the cross.

   ii) Under this covenant, God has placed all judgment (John 12:31-32) and punishment for all our past, present, and future sins on the Lord Jesus.

iii) He doesn't punish us anymore as He would under the Old Covenant. This New Covenant doesn't allow Him to do that. He is bound by this covenant that He made, and He doesn't violate it.

b) *"For the law was given by Moses, but grace and truth came by Jesus Christ."* –John 1:17

   i) Because of Jesus, who ushered in the New Covenant established on grace and truth, God deals with those under the New Covenant differently.

   ii) Not because He is indifferent but **because these are two different covenants that require two separate dealings**. This explains why God treated the folks in the Old Testament (OT) differently from the folks in the New Covenant.

   iii) With a closer look at the scriptures, you will see that God deals with people in three different ways in three different dispensations:

   - after the fall (before the Law was given)
   - after the Law was given
   - after Jesus' death and resurrection

   iv) God is not the one that changes or changed (Hebrews 13:5 and Malachi 3:6), but the people's behavior changed which was against the covenant they had entered into with God. Also, when the covenant changed, God changed the way He dealt with them, according to the New Covenant.

Let me explain:

After the fall
(Before the Law was given)

After the fall of man, God dealt with man based on grace. There was no law given, and therefore there was no sin imputed because where there is no law, sin is not imputed (Romans 5:13).

This does not mean that God was okay with the behavior of the people, but it means **He was not imputing their sins unto them**. *"Impute"* means *"to attribute responsibility for."* So, because God was not imputing sin unto them, holding them responsible for their sin, the people thought sin was okay. They had no idea what damage sin did to them. But sin was spreading rampantly like an epidemic (Genesis 6:5 "And GOD saw that the wickedness of man was great in the earth, and that every imagination of the thoughts of his heart was only evil continually," AND Genesis 19–Sodom and Gomorrah). Yet these people, before the law, thought nothing about it. Matter of fact, they thought they were godly. Because of all this, God had to install a temporary measure to:

a) Reveal God's standard of righteousness

b) Keep sin from spreading further and destroying humanity

During this time (dispensation), sin had no cure. Jesus had not come to die for the sins of the whole world yet. People could not be born again; it was impossible for this to happen without Jesus' finished work on the cross and it was premature for Jesus to come at this point.

So, God had to find a way to deal with the rampant spread of sin that was going to corrupt all of mankind and even hamper His big plan of Salvation that would later come through a virgin. **God started to judge people for their sins although the law had not been given yet.** This sounds strange because at this time it was a time of grace and God was not supposed to judge people or impute sins unto them because there was no law and they were not under the law, at least not yet.

In the effort to deal with the ruthless cancer (sin), God sent the flood and later brimstone and fire upon Sodom and Gomorrah. **God was not going to sit there and let the cancer of sin abort His entire plan of salvation by corrupting the whole human race.**

Two important aspects of God's judgement at this time before the law were:

a) **The Flood**

    i) *"And, behold, I, even I, do bring a flood of waters upon the earth, to destroy all flesh, wherein is the breath of life, from under heaven; and everything that is in the earth shall die."* –Genesis 6:17

    ii) *"Noah, Shem, Ham, Japheth, the sons of Noah, and Noah's wife, and the three wives of his sons with them, into the ark–these were spared and saved form the flood."* –Genesis 7:13

       • All people were destroyed except for Noah and his family

b) **Sodom and Gomorrah**

    i) "And the LORD *said, Because the cry of Sodom and Gomorrah is great, and because their sin is very grievous."* –Genesis 18:20

    ii) "Then the LORD *rained upon Sodom and upon Gomorrah brimstone and fire from the* LORD *out of heaven."* –Genesis 19:24

       • Lot and his two daughters were spared and saved from the judgment of Sodom and Gomorrah. –Genesis 19:30

Reasons God Sent the Flood:

a) **Sin was like a cancer that was out to destroy the entire body.** At this point, this cancer was at the leg working its way up to the head. What God did was to cut off or amputate the leg! This could stop the spread of cancer to the rest of the body. This act was quite barbaric and brutal to the leg and the person being amputated. However, by looking at the bigger picture, we can see that this act saved the life of this man. It's better to have no leg but be alive than to have one six feet under.

b) **The acts of judgment under the OT specifically before the law were an act of grace and mercy to mankind as a whole.** It saved the rest of mankind from the destructive cancer of sin that was aggressively reaching to plague and corrupt all. That said, we see the grace of God even in these acts that seemed so brutal. God was looking out for you and me, but it had a cost to some people. It's just like salvation; it cost God His Only Son (Jesus), but the result was that it paid for the sins of us all.

c) During the time before the law, like the time under the law, **God's judgment against evil was mercy to the rest of the people at large**. However, in the New Testament (NT), we can be delivered from the destructive cancer of sin. Because of Jesus and His finished work at the cross, the way God relates to us under the NT has changed.

After the Law
Why did God give the law; what was the purpose for the law?

a) After the first dispensation, *before and without the law*, God gave the law.

   i) Although the law was given, it was temporary. It was only for a season or for a specific period of time.

   ii) It was not God's best–the best was yet to come. I personally do not believe that God's heart was to give the law. If it was, why didn't He give it right away after the fall of man? I believe God's heart was grace from day one as we see it revealed after the law. God's heart was not to impute sin unto man. However, God had to change the way he dealt with mankind as man's behavior changed to combat the sin problem at hand.

   iii) He had to deal with the proliferation of sin.

b) Because man thought he was awesome, perfect, and godly, not in need of a savior, God gave the law to reveal His righteous standard to man.

i) The law showed man how impoverished he was, and his need of a savior.

ii) It blew all the blinders of deception off him because now he knew how ugly and ungodly, he was.

iii) It revealed all the ugliness of man. Man realized he was not as good as he thought once God's holy and righteous standard had been revealed.

"The law can still do the same to those who think they are so good and have no need of a savior." **–1 Timothy 1:8-10**

c) The way God turned away people from sin under the OT law was by bringing judgment on the sin through punishment.

i) When the law was given, it held people accountable for their sin.

ii) It did not set them free from sinning.

iii) It was like a mirror that showed them what was wrong, but it could not fix it.

iv) So, the law, to a degree, limited the dissemination of sin and revealed God's standard of righteousness.

v) The law was a part of God's plan for redemption, but it was only a temporary measure put in place until Jesus came (Galatians 3:23-25).

d) Contrary to what most people think, God did not give the law to be kept. If anything, it was the very opposite.

i) Some people think they can or have kept the law (Mark 10:17-23). Nothing can be further from the truth.

- The law couldn't be kept. It was powerless to justify even if one were to keep it. Justification couldn't come through the keeping of the law but by faith in the finished work of the cross.

ii) No one has ever kept the big Ten Commandments, let alone all the 613 laws in total.

iii) James 2:10 says that if you stumble in one law, you are guilty of breaking all.

iv) For one to truly keep the law he not only has to do the **outward** physical keeping of the law, but also the **inward** keeping of it. This was and is impossible.

v) The Law should drive anyone to surrender and give up. It is impossible to keep. Matter of fact, only Jesus (God) kept the whole law perfectly. There is not another person that could do it.

e) God gave the law to drive these people to the end of themselves and get them to give up trying to save themselves, and instead cry out for a Savior–Jesus.

i) He gave it to show people how sinful and unholy they were. The law showed people that they were sinful and incapable of keeping it through trying.

ii) **In simple terms, the Law empowered and strengthened our enemy, sin, not us.**

f) Why would God give us the Law to strengthen our enemy (sin)?

i) Sin had already defeated and beaten us, but we weren't aware of it.

ii) We were deceived in our thinking that we weren't so bad.

iii) We thought we were somewhat good. However, according to Romans 3:23, the Bible says that we all have sinned and come short of the glory of God. We were sinners, imperfect and unholy, although we thought we weren't.

g) To recap, the Bible says God gave the Law:

i) **To produce guilt and stop every mouth**

"Now we know that what things soever the law saith, it saith to them who are under the law: that every mouth may be stopped, and all the world may become guilty before God." – Romans 3:19

- **No one is to boast, after all, we have all come short.**

ii) **To give knowledge of sin**

"Therefore, by the deeds of the law there shall no flesh be justified in his sight: for by the law is the knowledge of sin." –Romans 3:20

- **Thereby revealing our need for the Savior by showing us how horrible we were.**

iii) **As a school master (tutor) to hold back the growth and spread of sin to a degree.**

"But before faith came, we were kept under the law, shut up unto the faith which should afterwards be revealed. Wherefore the law was our schoolmaster to bring us unto Christ, that we might be justified by faith. But after that faith is come, we are no longer under a schoolmaster." – Galatians 3:23-25

iv) **To strengthen sin**

"The sting of death is sin; and the strength of sin is the law." –1 Corinthians 15:56

- **So, we can surrender and call out for help from Jesus the Savior.**

v) **To deceive and slay**

"For sin, taking occasion by the commandment, deceived me, and by it slew me." – Romans 7:11

vi) **To condemn**

"For if the ministration of condemnation be glory, much more doth the ministration of righteousness exceed in glory." – 2 Corinthians 3:9

- **No one enjoys condemnation. The law will condemn you, thereby driving you to the Savior.**

vii) **To kill**

"Who also hath made us able ministers of the new testament; not of the letter, but of the spirit: for the letter killeth, but the spirit giveth life." –2 Corinthians 3:6

- **The law kills. Those who don't want to die would call out for help from the Savior.**

Important Considerations Regarding the Law Dispensation

A. The Law was mankind's infancy stage

a) The Law was like an infancy stage of mankind. At that point, reasoning could not work because mankind was an infant. You do not reason with an infant. Infancy calls for a different approach than maturity. All you need to do for a child or an infant to stop them from doing what is wrong is punish them. You have to say to an infant, "Do this and I will spank you." Infants understand that type of language. They cannot understand the reasoning language yet.

b) For instance, you can't tell them that if you do something wrong you are yielding to the devil, and you will reap bad things. They may not know about resisting the devil (James 4:7), but the truth is that when that thought of sin comes again, they will resist because they don't want to be spanked.

c) I believe this is the reason the Bible advocates spanking children (Proverbs 13:24; 19:18; 22:15; 23:13; 29:15; 29:17). Sometimes kids need to be spanked not to hurt them, but to deter them from doing what is **wrong until such a time as they can be reasoned with**.

    i) This works perfectly well but only up to a certain age.

    ii) Spanking is not a long-term solution.

    iii) You only use physical restraint for a short period of time until a child grows up and then you can teach them by instruction.

    iv) You do not spank an 18 or 20-year-old, but instead you reason or instruct him. Why? Because he is no longer an infant. He has matured and can be reasoned with.

d) Likewise, the OT revealed God's wrath against sin, and He put punishment in place to deter the Israelites (at an infant stage) from sinning until His plan of redemption could unfold.

    i) When the time was right, Jesus came and paid for our sin (Gal 3:24-25).

    ii) God dealt with sin harshly in order to keep the Israelites out of trouble.

    iii) The law limited and restricted sin, although it **could not completely stop it**.

    iv) The law was just a training tool God used to guide His children until they could be saved by faith. **Another way of saying this is that the human race was at its infancy stage until Jesus came and revealed the true nature of God.**

e) Under the Old Covenant there were very harsh punishments for sin.

  i) For example, God commanded to kill all the men, women, children, and even animals when they conquered other nations (Joshua 6:17:21, 10:40; 11:11-14).

  ii) Another command was for the Israelites to kill their own children if they were persistently stubborn and rebellious (Deuteronomy 21:18-21).

  iii) This is because, like the times of the flood and Sodom and Gomorrah, they couldn't be cured or healed. So, they were "taken out" of the society; in much the same way doctors cut out a cancerous tumor in an effort to save the rest of the body.

  iv) It wasn't possible for anyone to be born again, and God didn't want foreign people infecting the children of Israel with demonic beliefs or behavior which would further the sin instead of limiting it.

B. The Israelites agreed to do all in the Old Covenant.

"And all the people answered together, and said, All that the LORD hath spoken we will do. And Moses returned the words of the people unto the LORD."
                                                                        –Exodus 19:8

"And Moses came and told the people all the words of the LORD, and all the judgments: and all the people answered with one voice, and said, All the words which the LORD hath said will we do. And he took the book of the covenant and read in the audience of the people: and they said, all that the LORD hath said will we do, and be obedient."
                                                                    –Exodus 24:3, 7

a) *"Now therefore, if ye will obey my voice indeed, and keep my covenant, then ye shall be a peculiar treasure unto me above all people: for all the earth is mine: And ye shall be unto me a kingdom of priests, and an holy nation. These are the words which thou shalt speak unto the children of Israel."* –Exodus 19:5-6

i) God promised the children of Israel that they would be to Him a peculiar treasure above all people.

ii) The people agreed to God's words.

iii) God then proceeded to give the law to Moses with the blessings and the judgments.

iv) Moses read the words of the Lord and the judgments, and the people agreed to the covenant.

v) In Exodus 24:7, they again agreed to the covenant. In so doing, they authorized God to fulfill the words of His covenant with them.

vi) They were to be blessed for obedience and cursed for disobedience (Deuteronomy 28).

b) **Each disobedience from the children of Israel obligated God to act accordingly. They had a covenant and He had to act based on that covenant. He had given His Word and the people had given their word.**

i) God is not the author of evil. Israel's disobedience to God released the judgment of the Old Covenant.

ii) Under the OT God's judgment against evil was mercy to the rest of the body, but in the NT, we can be delivered from sin. Because of Jesus, the way God relates to us under the NT has changed.

Under Grace

a) Unlike under the Law which came by Moses, the New Covenant of grace and truth came by Christ Jesus (John 1:17).

i) The death and resurrection of Jesus ushered in the New Covenant– the covenant of grace, not of law and performance.

ii) This covenant is totally dependent on Jesus and His finished work at the cross.

iii) This covenant enabled us to be born again (saved), which in return removed and stopped all judgment and imputing of sin on us, because Jesus took our judgement (John 12:31) and all our sin was imputed on Him.

b) At this stage, mankind is at **maturity**.

   i) God doesn't spank us or punish us anymore. He reasons with us because we can be born again.

   ii) Although spanking was effective during mankind's infancy, it is no longer applicable, and its role has come to an end.

c) Under the NT, our sins have been paid for by Jesus and God isn't holding sin against us anymore.

   i) God has changed the way He deals with us because the price of sin has been paid.

   ii) This single event made us brand new (2 Corinthians 5:17, Hebrews 8:12-13).

   iii) Jesus changed how God relates to and deals with us–forever.

   iv) Jesus revealed God in a way that **superseded** all previous revelations (Hebrews 1:3).

   v) The revelation of God had been progressive up until Jesus. Jesus is the complete revelation of God the Father (John 14:3-9, Col 2:9).

d) **Illustration 1: Jesus shows mercy to the woman caught in adultery (John 8:1-11)**

   i) Under the law this woman caught in adultery would have been stoned to death (Lev 20:10; Deuteronomy 22:22), however, we see a totally different approach in the New Testament.

    ii) Jesus showed her grace and mercy instead of judgment.

    iii) God was already dealing with people differently because of the difference Jesus made. Jesus brought grace and truth, not law and judgement (John 1:17).

    iv) He also said all law and prophets prophesied until John the Baptist (Matthew 11:13).

e) Adultery is wrong (Proverbs 6:24-33) and Jesus was not excusing or condoning her sin. However, the way God deals with mankind under the New Testament has changed because of Jesus.

    i) Sin is no longer imputed unto people.

    ii) In this instance, Jesus was going to take all the judgment and the sin of this woman.

    iii) It is astonishing to see that the Pharisees and the scribes brought only the woman that they said was caught in the very act of adultery. Where is the man that was involved in this adulterous relationship? If she was caught in the very act, then the man must have been present along with this woman. **These scribes and Pharisees were not seeking justice because the man was not brought before Jesus**. I tend to think that this hidden man was one of them–a Pharisee or a Sadducee.

    iv) They wanted to trap Jesus in front of the multitude because a woman would invoke more sympathy than the man so; by playing the "woman card" it would serve their plans better.

f) Unlike the harsh, judgmental, legalistic message of the Pharisees, scribes, and Sadducees, people knew Jesus as the **gracious one**, not the judging one.

    i) He had been teaching grace and forgiveness towards sinners. Agreeing to stone this woman would have sent a totally contradicting message. Any contrary action would have blown His testimony and reputation.

    ii) These Pharisees wanted to destroy Jesus, and this was a good opportunity for pushing their narrative that "Jesus condoned and practiced sin by His association with the sinners, breaking Jewish traditions such as Sabbaths." However, every time, Jesus successfully tamed every attack into a victory for the side of grace and mercy. Here these religious men thought they had Him "cornered" or trapped, and in their minds, they thought He was faced with only two options: to either condone her sin or to condemn her. Little did they know that God had option three: **"He that is without sin among you, let him first cast a stone at her."**

g) If Jesus held His teaching of forgiveness and refused to stone this woman, He would be in direct opposition to the Law of Moses (Lev 20:10) hence giving the Jews legal grounds to kill Him.

    i) If Jesus stoned the woman as says the law, then the people would forsake Him and not trust Him anymore. They would have seen Him just like the Pharisees.

    ii) The Pharisees believed that Jesus was trapped. They probably thought, "Here we go Jesus, let's see if You can come out of this trap. We got you cornered." No, He wasn't cornered because the foolishness of God is wiser than men (1Corinthians 1:25). Jesus rose to the occasion as always.

    iii) **Notice that He did not condone the sin or disregard the Law of Moses.** He simply told the one without sin to cast the first stone at her (John 8:7).

h) Why did Jesus not allow the stoning of this woman?

    i) He was simply forgiving this woman because **"all the prophets and the law prophesied until John" (Matthew 11:13)**.

ii) Jesus was operating under the dispensation of grace (John 1:17; Ephesians 3:2), not the law. **Jesus operated in the superior Law of grace, not the Law of works.**

iii) If anyone could rightfully stone this woman, it would have been Jesus because He was sinless, not the Sadducees, Scribes, and Pharisees.

i) Under our new and better covenant (Hebrews 8:6, 13), we don't kill our rebellious children or people who have sinned and are committing ungodly acts because, unlike in the OT, they can be born again and changed.

2 Corinthians 5:17-19 says, *"Therefore if any man be in Christ, he is a new creature: old things are passed away; behold, all things are become new. And all things are of God, who hath reconciled us to himself by Jesus Christ, and hath given to us the ministry of reconciliation; To wit, that God was in Christ, reconciling the world unto himself, not imputing their trespasses unto them; and hath committed unto us the word of reconciliation."*

After we accept Jesus and make Him the Lord of our lives, the following happens:

i) We become new creatures.

ii) We are reconciled to God. The word *"reconcile"* means to make or bring two or more opposing parties at peace or friends again.

iii) God does NOT impute sin unto us. God did not charge sin to our account.

- David saw this very thing (God not imputing sins unto us) and prophesied about it over a thousand years before Jesus. He said, *"Blessed is the man unto whom the LORD imputeth not iniquity, and in whose spirit there is no guile."* –Psalms 32:2

- God took away all the punishment and separation that sin caused, and He harmonized our relationship with Him again.

God took the sins of all humanity and charged it to the account of Jesus–His own account (2 Corinthians 5:21). Thank You, Jesus. Hallelujah!

j) **Illustration 2: Luke 9:51-54 (Samaritans, Jesus, and the disciples).**

   i) In this story, the Samaritans **refused to allow Jesus into their city because He was going to Jerusalem.**

   ii) The Samaritans hated the Jews down in Jerusalem and anyone who associated with them.

   iii) When the disciples saw this rejection, they were not impressed. They asked Jesus if they could **call down fire from heaven to burn these Samaritans** as Prophet Elijah had done earlier in the Old Testament (2 Kings 1:3-4).

   iv) Jesus' response was off the charts.

   v) He responded with grace and mercy for the Samaritans while rebuking His disciples.

   vi) He said in Luke 9:55-56, *"Ye know not what manner of spirit ye are of. For the Son of man is not come to destroy men's lives, but to save them. And they went to another village."*

k) Again, Jesus dealt with these Samaritans based on the **New Covenant of grace**. Had this been the Old Testament, the results would have been totally different.

   i) Additionally, the Samaritans' rejection of Jesus was much worse than anything the army captains and their soldiers did to Elijah (2 Kings 1).

   ii) **The Lord did not come to destroy lives but to save them.**

   iii) **How could He save those He was to destroy?**

l) Once you truly understand **the significance and magnitude of Jesus' sacrifice, then you can understand why God dealt with people differently under the New Covenant than He did under the Old Testament**.

    i) Under the Old Testament, the payment for our sins had not been made and people's sins were imputed unto them. **However, Jesus' coming to the earth made a pivotal difference in the way God dealt and deals with mankind.**

    God always desired to relate to us by grace, but He couldn't under the OT because of humanity's hardness of heart and the inability to be born again.

In conclusion, although under the New Covenant God is not punishing us, judging our sins or imputing them unto us, the **consequences of sin** have not gone away and they are not a punishment from God. Sin has already been dealt with in full, but:

a) **The consequences of sin still apply.**

b) **The law of sowing and reaping is still in full effect.** *"Be not deceived; God is not mocked: for whatsoever a man soweth, that shall he also reap. For* **he that soweth to his flesh shall of the flesh reap corruption**; *but he that soweth to the Spirit shall of the Spirit reap life everlasting."* (Galatians 6:7-8 emphasis mine).

    i) I just want to point out that this verse says of the **FLESH we reap corruption, not of GOD**. The natural horizontal consequences of sin will still occur although the vertical consequences that hindered our relationship with Jesus and separated us from God have been taken care of once for all.

Chapter Three

Who Is a Christian and Who Is a Disciple? What is the Difference Between a Believer in Jesus and a Disciple of Jesus?

A convert is not synonymous with a disciple. There is a clear distinction between the two. Every disciple is a convert first, but not every convert becomes a disciple. Most believers think they are disciples of Jesus because they are believers. Nothing can be further from the truth.

Discipleship and Conversion

a) There is a huge difference between being a Christian convert and a disciple. I will explain this difference in this chapter. **Every Christian is a convert, but not every Christian is a disciple**. Anyone can become a convert but not a disciple. We can do better evangelism through discipleship than the way it's done today.

b) This is one of the reasons that our society is going in the wrong direction–**there is a lack of discipleship**.

c) For instance, a disciple does not vote for a person, but for the Bible (biblical values and principles). A convert on-the-other-hand, votes for people, emotions, charisma, looks, education, skin color, etc.

d) God's Word has a lot to say about the issues we face today in all societies, but for us to have an impact on our societies, we must graduate to being disciples, instead of just converts.

e) Through God's Word, we must develop a biblical worldview, approach, and perspective on all things and speak up.

    i) We ought to be the light of the world and the salt of the earth–and one of the best ways to be effective in that is to study and continue in God's Word.

    ii) **We should develop a discipleship mentality, not a convert mentality.**

"You can be a believer and a liberal, but you can't be a disciple and a liberal."

–Andrew Wommack.

A sincere repeating of a sinner's prayer does not make you a disciple, but a convert or a believer in Jesus Christ. Being a disciple of Jesus is more than a *"fire insurance policy prayer"* of salvation. Salvation isn't just about getting our foot in the door.

I like to explain the difference between a disciple and a convert like this: a disciple is a mature Christian believer, while a convert is an immature Christian. Most importantly, I want to stress that I don't say all this to offend but to draw out a distinction between the two.

The heart of the Lord is to make disciples

God never commissioned us to go out and make converts, but to make disciples. A disciple is a born-again person who observes all things that Jesus commanded.

Matthew 28:19-20 says, *"Go ye therefore, and **teach all nations**, baptizing them in the name of the Father, and of the Son, and of the Holy Ghost: Teaching them to **observe all things** whatsoever I have commanded you: and, lo, I am with you always, even unto the end of the world. Amen."*

The NIV says, *"Therefore, go and **make disciples** of all nations, baptizing them in the name of the Father and of the Son and of the Holy Spirit, and teaching them to obey everything I have commanded you. And surely I am with you always, to the very end of the age."*

The key points to these verses are:

a) Make disciples.

   The primary way we make disciples is through teaching. Teaching is the foundation of making disciples. It is one thing to proclaim the truth, it is another thing to teach it.

b) Teach them to **observe all things**.

   The discipleship process is where we teach believers to observe all things that pertain to the kingdom of God.

c) The word *"Disciple"* also means:

   i)   A learner

   ii) A pupil

   iii) Imitator

   iv) To go on or continue

   v)   It is in this word "disciple", that we get the word "discipline." **So, a disciple is a disciplined follower of the Lord Jesus.**

Below are some of the characteristics of a disciple:

A. Loves others

"By this shall all men know that ye are my disciples, if ye have love one to another."

–John 13:35

a) One of the main characteristics of true disciples is that they **love each other**.

b) Loving one another is a sign or proof that one is a disciple or a mature follower of the Lord Jesus.

B. Bears much fruit

> *"Herein is my Father glorified, that ye bear much fruit; so shall ye be my disciples. As the Father hath loved me, so have I loved you: continue ye in my love."*
>
> –John 15:8-9

a) A disciple is one that bears fruit. Until we move on to the level of being disciples, we can't bear fruit.

C. Has fruit that remains

> *"Ye have not chosen me, but I have chosen you, and ordained you, that **ye should go and bring forth fruit, and that your fruit should remain**: that whatsoever ye shall ask of the Father in my name, he may give it you."*
>
> –John 15:16 (emphasis mine)

a) It is one thing to bear fruit, but it is another thing altogether for that fruit to remain (stay). The fruit of the disciple MUST REMAIN. There is need of consistency. A disciple can be seen not only by the fruit they bear, but by their consistency as well.

D. Keeps a commitment to the Lord above anything else

a) *"And a man's foes shall be they of his own household. He that loveth father or mother more than me is not worthy of me: and he that loveth son or daughter more than me is not worthy of me."* –Matthew 10:36-37

   "If any man come to me, and hate not his father, and mother, and wife, and children, and brethren, and sisters, yea, and his own life also, he cannot be my disciple." –Luke 14:26-27

   i) A true disciple will be willing to give up **all** for the Lord.

ii) Choosing to follow Jesus is a costly decision. Many believers in Jesus aren't willing or ready to give up their father, mother, wife, children, brethren, sisters, and their own lives.

- **This means they are not ready and cannot be disciples.**

iii) **Salvation is free, but discipleship will cost you everything!**

b) *"But Jesus did not commit himself unto them, because he knew all men."* –John 2:24

i) Notice Jesus refused to commit His ministry to converts. They weren't disciples. They were immature and undependable.

ii) There has been huge damage done in and by the church by people who are converts, rather than disciples.

- There is more to ministry than being born again.
- **We must disciple people and NOT just make converts.**

c) *"Not a novice, lest being lifted up with pride he fall into the condemnation of the devil."* –1 Timothy 3:6

i) This means a *novice* could not qualify.

ii) A novice is defined by Strong's concordance as *"newly planted that is (figuratively) a young convert"*.

iii) Although a young convert might be excited about things of God, he is not the best witness because of a lack maturity and depth.

- Once persecution arises, they tend to buckle because of a lack of depth.

Your commitment to the Lord will be tested by this life. Everything you believe will come to a test, sooner or later.

E. Endures hardship

A believer or convert can live without suffering persecution, but a disciple can't escape persecution.

a) *"Thou therefore, my son, be strong in the grace that is in Christ Jesus. And the things that thou hast heard of me among many witnesses, the same commit thou to faithful men, who shall be able to teach others also. Thou therefore endure hardness, as a good soldier of Jesus Christ. No man that warreth entangleth himself with the affairs of this life; that he may please him who hath chosen him to be a soldier."* –2 Timothy 2:1-4.

   i) Paul was very careful and selective in his instructions as to who to commit these truths to.

   ii) He never committed those things that were taught by him to anyone, but to the believers who were "able to **teach**" and were "**faithful men**."

   • These believers being described by Paul are exactly equivalent to the description of a disciple—mature, able to teach, and faithful.

   iii) Additionally, a disciple is one who endures hardness like a soldier. A true disciple will not easily buckle while under persecution or pressure. He endures it. He doesn't give up whatever the circumstances may be.

b) *"Yea, and all that will live godly in Christ Jesus shall suffer persecution."* –2 Timothy 3:12

   i) I'm convinced that believers or converts hardly live godly lives; it's the **disciples** who **aspire to live godly lives**.

F. Continues in the Word

You must continue in the Word of God if you are going to be His disciple. This ought to be the main goal for every single Christian.

"As he spake these words, many believed on him. Then said Jesus to those Jews which believed on him, If ye continue in my word, then are ye my disciples indeed; And ye shall know the truth, and the truth shall make you free."

–John 8:30-32

a) Notice here in these verses that Jesus was speaking to **those that had believed on Him** (believers).

    i) These people were already believers, but they weren't disciples yet, so, Jesus told them how to become disciples.

b) A true disciple must continue in the Word. This is not a one-time thing, but a continual process.

    i) A lack of consistency in the Word of God is a clear indication that one is not a disciple, but a convert.

c) You are to continue until you **know the truth** so that the **truth you now know makes you free**.

    i) The Truth will not just set you free but will make you free.

    ii) Yet, furthermore, it is the truth that you know and have a revelation of that will make you free.

d) Being a believer is not all there is to relationship with God.

    i) Conversion is not enough. Going to church one hour a week will not cut it. **You need discipline, quality, and quantity time!**

    ii) You must continue in the Word that it begins to reshape your thinking, lifestyle, morality, philosophy, politics, opinions, values, and beliefs.

      iii) A person that will believe contrary to the Word of God, holding opposing values to the Word for emotional reasons is not a disciple. A disciple will let the Word of God shape what they believe.

e) **Take time to mature, grow, and continue in the Word.**

      i) If you are not a disciple, you have little to no business representing God because all you will do is misrepresent Him.

      ii) You will cause more harm and damage than good. You need to take time to mature, grow, and continue in the Word.

      iii) A disciple must be mature and be able to represent God properly, accurately, while rightly dividing the Word of Truth.

f) *"And they continued steadfastly in the apostles' doctrine and fellowship, and in breaking of bread, and in prayers." –Acts 2:42*

      i) The apostles did not lead people into conversion. They discipled them! They continued teaching and discipling with the apostles' doctrine.

      ii) *"And daily in the temple, and in every house, they ceased not to teach and preach Jesus Christ." –Acts 5:42*

      iii) Paul taught everywhere in every church (1 Corinthians 4:17).

G. Receives directly from the Lord

a) God never intended things to be the way they are. He never intended only the fivefold ministry to be the only provision to the entire body of Christ. A continual dependence on the *"super-dupers"* is the reason we haven't evangelized the world yet.

      i) This dependence is the reason that we have so many immature believers and not disciples.

ii) Believers should mature and become disciples to the point that they do not need the pastor or apostle to have their needs met. They should be able to hear and receive from God by themselves, and not be dependent on the church leadership and clergy.

iii) Ephesians 4:11 clearly states that the fivefold ministry is to equip, furnish, disciple, and perfect **the saints to do the work of the ministry**.

- It's not meant for the fivefold to do the work of the ministry. This has been a disservice to the body of Christ.

iv) The ultimate goal of preaching the gospel should be discipleship, not conversion.

- True, conversion is the first step towards discipleship, but we should go beyond that to discipleship.
- You can hardly find evidence to convict a convert for being a Christian, **but you will find plenty of evidence to convict a disciple for being a Christian**.
- The same way a person gives birth to a baby and doesn't throw away or abandon that baby but feeds, nurtures, and helps mature her, we should do the same with all the converts.

Steps to becoming a disciple:

a) **Make Jesus your Lord and Christ**

The first thing in becoming a disciple is your relationship with Jesus as your Savior. Yet, there is more.

You cannot be a disciple if you are not willing to make Jesus the absolute LORD and Master over everything in your life. He must be Lord over everything. You must make a total commitment to the LORD, if not you will continue to struggle in life. Becoming a disciple is the way to go to move forward.

*"Therefore, let all the house of Israel know assuredly, that God hath made that same Jesus, whom ye have crucified, both **Lord and Christ.**"*

–Acts 2:36

    i) A believer is someone who has made Jesus their Savior, but not the Lord of their daily life, while a disciple is one who has made Jesus both Savior and Lord.

- **Every believer should aspire to make Jesus the Lord of their life and should live accordingly.**

    ii) When someone is your lord, he is your master. The word "lord" means one having power and authority over others; a ruler by preeminence to whom service and obedience are due.

    iii) The Lord ought to be the one calling the shots, not you.

b) **Desire and hunger for the Word**

    i) *"Wherefore laying aside all malice, and all guile, and hypocrisies, and envies, and all evil speakings, as newborn babes, desire the sincere milk of the word, that ye may grow thereby."* –1 Peter 2:1-2

    ii) Many people have been born again for years, but they have been baby Christians ever since.

- They have never grown or matured. Although they are counting the years they have been born again, they are Christian babies with an old age number.
- If you aren't a disciple, it's best to stay away from ministry. You will end up doing more harm than good to the body of Christ and/or the unbelievers. What are you sharing or teaching that you don't know about?

    iii) I have heard many unbelievers that were turned off by certain Christians they encountered and mostly because these believers were immature believers.

- I remember a story about Mahatma Gandhi that he went to a Presbyterian church to give his life to the Lord Jesus Christ and he was turned away because of the color of his skin. He then said, *"I would have been a Christian, if I had never met one."*

- He further said, *"I like your Christ; I do not like your Christians. Your Christians are so unlike your Christ."* So, would you say that these believers were disciples? No, I wouldn't.

c) Discover your purpose, call, and giftings

"And he gave some, apostles; and some, prophets; and some, evangelists; and some, pastors and teachers; For the perfecting of the saints, for the work of the ministry, for the edifying of the body of Christ: Till we all come in the unity of the faith, and of the knowledge of the Son of God, unto a perfect man, unto the measure of the stature of the fulness of Christ: That we henceforth be no more children, tossed to and fro, and carried about with every wind of doctrine, by the sleight of men, and cunning craftiness, whereby they lie in wait to deceive."

–Ephesians 4:11-14

i) **This a very crucial point of discipleship. This is where you learn to be faithful and discover your purpose, call, and gifting.**

  - Faithfulness precedes being a minister and being put in the ministry.

    - Before we are called in the ministry, we need to be faithful first.
    - 2 Timothy 2:1-2–God equips and enables the faithful.
    - 1 Corinthians 4:2–Faithfulness can be found.
    - 1 Timothy 1:12–Faithfulness can be counted down to how many times one has been faithful.

ii) Considering a fivefold calling/ministry?

- God will call you to the fivefold ministry even though you are still a convert or a baby Christian believer, but **He will not separate you to that work and office of the ministry until you have become a disciple**.
- A convert cannot edify, perfect, nor equip the saints for the work of the ministry. Only a disciple can do that, not a just convert or believer.

d) **Study to show thyself approved unto God**

"Study to shew thyself approved unto God, a workman that needeth not to be ashamed, rightly dividing the word of truth."

–2 Timothy 2:15

i) The word *study* here is not referring to acquiring knowledge through reading, but rather is talking about *"make haste, to exert oneself, endeavor"* (Thayer's Greek English).

ii) Until we graduate from being converts to disciples, we are not able to rightly divide the word of truth. It is a characteristic of an immature believer to wrongly divide the Word of Truth.

- Notice that it all starts with one making haste or being diligent to show ourselves approved unto God. This happens as we continue in the Word of God (John 8:30-33).

e) **Know the truth and be made free**

"As he spake these words, many believed on him. Then said Jesus to those Jews which believed on him, If ye continue in my word, then are ye my disciples indeed; And ye shall know the truth, and the truth shall make you free."

–John 8:30-32

i) Are you free from bondage? If you are not, you are probably not a disciple, at least not yet.

- Most people commonly say that the truth shall set you free, but that is not a true statement.

- How many people do you know that know the truth, yet they aren't free? I bet you can name many that can tell you the truth and quote it word for word.

- It is because it is the truth that you continue in that will make you free.

ii) **When we continue in the Word, we get a revelation of the truth and that truth that we now know MAKES us free. Only disciples will become truly free.**

f) **Continue in the Word**

"As he spake these words, many believed on him. Then said Jesus to those Jews which believed on him, If ye continue in my word, then are ye my disciples indeed; And ye shall know the truth, and the truth shall make you free."

–John 8:30-32

i) *"Thy word is a lamp unto my feet, and a light unto my path."* –Psalm 119:105

- If we need light and good vision, we need the Word of God. We can't see our path without light, God's Word is that light.

ii) *"The entrance of thy words giveth light; it giveth understanding unto the simple."* –Psalm 119:130

- If we want understanding, it comes from the Word of God. A lack of understanding is a sign of the absence of the Word of God because it is that which brings light and understanding.

iii) *"But be ye doers of the word, and not hearers only, deceiving your own selves. For if any be a hearer of the word, and not a doer, he is like unto a man beholding his natural face in a glass: For he beholdeth himself, and goeth his way, and straightway forgetteth what manner of man he* was. But whoso **looketh** into the perfect law of liberty, and **continueth therein**, he being not a forgetful hearer, but a doer of the work, this man shall be blessed in his deed." –James 1:22-25

- **Be a doer and continue therein**
- Some of the key determinations of whether we are converts, believers, or disciples lies in whether **we are doers of the Word**, not on how much we know and the head knowledge we possess.
  - One of the ways we do the Word is by believing on the Lord Jesus (John 6:28-29)
- These verses further emphasize the need to not just look into the Word but continue in it. We can't just do it one time.
  - If we are going to mature and become disciples and doers of the Word, we ought to continue in it. The key is in continuing. We just should not stop.

g) **Take heed to the Word of God**

"Wherewithal shall a young man cleanse his way? by taking heed thereto according to thy word. With my whole heart have I sought thee: O let me not wander from thy commandments. Thy word have I hid in mine heart, that I might not sin against thee."

–Psalm 119:9-11

i) Disciples have a desire to take heed (apply themselves) to the Word of God which in return cleanses their ways. So, we can safely say that if the Word of God has not cleansed our way, it is because we have not taken heed to it.

h) **Renew your mind**

"I beseech you therefore, brethren, by the mercies of God, that ye present your bodies a living sacrifice, holy, acceptable unto God, which is your

reasonable service. And be not conformed to this world: but be ye trans-
formed by the renewing of your mind, that ye may prove what is that good,
and acceptable, and perfect, will of God."

–Romans 12:1-2

i)   If you have not aligned your thinking according to God's Word, nor allowed the Word of God to shape, change, or get in the way of what you believe, most likely you aren't a disciple.

ii) You ought to let the Word of God change your opinions, beliefs, values, philosophy, and outlook on life.

   • If we do not renew our minds, we will stay conformed to this world and we will miss out on knowing the good, acceptable, and perfect will of God.

   • A true disciple will be transformed by the renewing of his mind by the Word of God.

Without being born again, you cannot become a disciple. Without making Jesus the Lord of your daily life and without the desire for the Word of God, there is no growth. Without the knowing the Word of God, there is no freedom. Without continuing in the Word of God there is no maturity and stability. And, without taking heed and acting on it, there are no results and no fruit.

Additional Points About Discipleship

A. Example of True Discipleship: Jesus Feeding Thousands

"And when the day was now far spent, his disciples came unto him, and said, This is a desert place, and now the time is far passed: Send them away, that they may go into the country round about, and into the villages, and buy themselves bread: for they have nothing to eat. He answered and said unto them, Give ye them to eat. And they say unto him, Shall we go and buy two hundred pennyworth of bread, and give them to eat? He saith unto

them, how many loaves have ye? go and see. And when they knew, they say, five, and two fishes. And he commanded them to make all sit down by companies upon the green grass. And they sat down in ranks, by hundreds, and by fifties. And when he had taken the five loaves and the two fishes, he looked up to heaven, and blessed, and broke the loaves, and gave them to his disciples to set before them; and the two fishes divided he among them all. And they did all eat, and were filled. And they took up twelve baskets full of the fragments, and of the fishes. And they that did eat of the loaves were about five thousand men. And straightway he constrained his disciples to get into the ship, and to go to the other side before unto Bethsaida, while he sent away the people."

–Mark 6:35-45 and Matthew 14:13-23

a) Jesus demonstrated and proved that discipleship is the way to meet the needs of the people.

    i) **Multiplication of the bread happened in the hands of the disciples** as they passed it out to the multitude, not while in the hands of Jesus.

    ii) If we are going to make a huge difference, this is the best way to go to evangelize the world effectively.

b) Jesus also spent twice as much time teaching as he spent preaching.

    i) Teaching explains truth and how to walk in it.

    ii) Teaching is more than just proclaiming the truth.

B. Exceptions to Discipleship in the Word

There are only two **exceptions** to discipleship in the Scriptures and they are an exception, not the general rule.

a) Man on the cross (Luke 23:42-43)

- The man on the cross had no time to be discipled. He was on a death penalty.

b) Ethiopian eunuch (Acts 8)

    i)   In the situation of the Ethiopian eunuch, Phillip was sent by the Lord to minister salvation to this man and then was removed from him.

    ii) This eunuch was not discipled, but usually this is not the case.

C. More to Discipleship

As much as teaching is the primary way to disciple people, there is more to it than that. These verses show that in addition to teaching, one must set an example for others in: doctrine, longsuffering, manner of life, purpose, faith, charity, patience, afflictions and persecutions, purity, in word, and in spirit in order for a person to be entirely discipled.

a) 2 Timothy 3:10-11 "But thou hast fully known my doctrine, manner of life, purpose, faith, longsuffering, charity, patience, persecutions, afflictions, which came unto me at Antioch, at Iconium, at Lystra; what persecutions I endured: but out of *them* all the Lord delivered me."

    i)   Notice that Paul said that Timothy had fully, not partially known his doctrine, manner of life, purpose, faith, longsuffering, charity, patience, persecutions, afflictions.

    ii) All these portray more of a person's whole life rather than just teaching.

b) 2 Timothy 4:2 "Preach the word; be instant in season, out of season; reprove, rebuke, exhort with all longsuffering and doctrine."

c) 1 Timothy 4:12-13 "Let no man despise thy youth; but be thou an example of the believers, in word, in conversation, in charity, in spirit, in faith, in purity. Till I come, give attendance to reading, to exhortation, to doctrine."

D. "The four Gospels refer to Jesus teaching forty-three times and preaching nineteen times, and four verses refer to Him preaching and teaching in the same verse. This would indicate that Jesus spent twice as much time teaching as He did preaching. Teaching is the basic building block of making disciples. Jesus was making disciples, not just converts."–Note 3 on Matthew 5:2 in Andrew Wommack's *Living Commentary*.

There was a time when most churches had Sunday schools that discipled believers. This has changed quite a bit. Discipleship is a missing ingredient in the body of Christ that would bring about the level of maturity that is missing in the body.

Chapter Four

Who Is the Author or Cause of Disease and Sickness?

We can't clearly address this question without talking about the creation account first. The best way to understand who is the author of sickness, disease, and all these physical challenges is to look at creation and the original state of things.

In the beginning, God created the heavens and the earth. In everything God created, He said, "It was good." Sickness and disease were never a part of it. Everything God created was good, in order, and perfectly complete.

"And the LORD God took the man, and put him into the garden of Eden to dress it and to keep it. And the LORD God commanded the man, saying, Of every tree of the garden thou mayest freely eat: But of the tree of the knowledge of good and evil, thou shalt not eat of it: for in the day that thou eatest thereof thou shalt surely die."

–Genesis 2:15-17

When God created man, He put him in the garden to keep it. He also gave him a command to not eat of the tree of the knowledge of good and evil. When man disobeyed and ate of that tree, their sin produced and released death into the earth and all the creation that God had made. So, because of this sin, a door was opened to every mess, death, and corruption you can imagine such as death, old age, corruption, sickness, disease, deformities, and on and on the list goes.

The first point I want to make is that God had nothing to do with the way things transpired as a result of man's sins. It would be wrong and inaccurate to blame God for what man caused. Man was responsible for the mess that happened along with Satan who tempted him. In other words, the combination of man and Satan ushered in the sickness and disease that we see today in the world–not God.

a) *"The thief cometh not, but for to steal, and to kill, and to destroy: I am come that they might have life, and that they might have it more abundantly."*–John 10:10

Satan is one of the main reasons we experience stealing, killing, and destroying.

i) Look no further, this verse among many others clearly spells out who kills, steals, and destroys. Satan is the thief, killer, and destroyer– NOT God. The devil is a main reason that bad things happen.

ii) Every tragedy, sickness, disease, death, and so forth can be categorized into these three things–stealing, killing, and destruction. If there is any stealing, killing, and destruction it is Satan (Devil) who is behind it–NOT God.

b) *"How art thou fallen from heaven, O Lucifer, son of the morning! How art thou cut down to the ground, which didst weaken the nations! For thou hast said in thine heart, I will ascend into heaven, I will exalt my throne above the stars of God: I will sit also upon the mount of the congregation, in the sides of the north: I will ascend above the heights of the clouds; I will be like the most High. Yet thou shalt be brought down to hell, to the sides of the pit. They that see thee shall narrowly look upon thee, and consider thee, saying, Is this the man that made the earth to tremble, that did shake kingdoms; That made the world as a wilderness, and destroyed the cities thereof; that opened not the house of his prisoners?"* –Isaiah 14:12-17

These verses talk about Lucifer who is well known as Satan. These verses clearly show that Satan or Lucifer is the one responsible for the evil and tragedy happening in the world. He has taken advantage of the fall of man and the corruption of sin and has exploited it, causing all sorts of damage.

They say he:

    i)   Made the world a wilderness

    ii) Destroyed cities

    iii) Imprisoned people (spiritually and physically)

This flies in the face of those who say God is the one who causes evil and tragedy. These verses clearly say that it is Lucifer (Satan)–NOT God.

c) *"And, behold, there was a woman which had a spirit of infirmity eighteen years, and was bowed together, and could in no wise lift up herself. And when Jesus saw her, he called her to him, and said unto her, Woman, thou art loosed from thine infirmity. And he laid his hands on her: and immediately she was made straight, and glorified God. And the ruler of the synagogue answered with indignation, because that Jesus had healed on the Sabbath day, and said unto the people, there are six days in which men ought to work: in them therefore come and be healed, and not on the Sabbath day. The Lord then answered him, and said, Thou hypocrite, doth not each one of you on the Sabbath loose his ox or his ass from the stall, and lead him away to watering? And ought not this woman, being a daughter of Abraham, whom* **Satan hath bound,** *lo, these eighteen years, be loosed from this bond on the Sabbath day?"* –Luke 13:11-16*

    i)   Here in these passages of scripture, we see Jesus healing a woman who had her back bent over (spine disease) for 38 years. He said that she was **bound by Satan,** meaning that Satan had put her in this state of misery, sickness, and disease for these 38 years. This is very telling of who the source of sickness and disease is. Obviously, it is Satan, not God.

d) *"How God anointed Jesus of Nazareth with the Holy Ghost and with power: who went about doing good, and healing all that were oppressed of the devil; for God was with him." –Acts 10:32*

   i) In this verse Peter summarizes the ministry of Jesus and says that He was going about place to place healing **all** that were oppressed of the devil–not of God.

     • He would not heal people if He was the one behind the sickness itself. He would be going against Himself.

   ii) People are oppressed of the devil, not of God. Satan is the main source of sickness, disease, and oppression.

e) *"He that committeth sin is of the devil; for the devil sinneth from the beginning. For this purpose the Son of God was manifested, that he might destroy the works of the devil." –1 John 3:8*

   i) Jesus came to destroy the works of the devil just as Acts 10:38 says, including sickness and diseases.

   ii) He was not destroying what He was for and authored.

It is simply error for some to assume or even proclaim that God is behind sickness and diseases. When we do not know the Lord nor His Word, we are in error (Matthew 22:29).

Chapter Five

Is Believing or Faith Alone the ONLY Requirement for Salvation? Is Water Baptism or Living Holy a Requirement for Salvation?

Most people think or believe that it is their good works and performance that produces salvation. However, the scriptures teach clearly that salvation is received only by faith in the finished work of the Lord Jesus plus nothing else. It is not faith plus our performance or good works.

Unlike all other religions, Christianity is not about performance and good deeds to earn salvation, favor, and the love of God. It teaches that no man can be good enough; therefore, all men need a savior. We can't perform nor work ourselves into the love of God, the blessing of God, and heaven because we can't do it perfectly. Even if you are better than me and your neighbor combined you still come short of the set standard of God. **God's standard is 100%. If you make 99.99% you have failed, even if you are better than the guy with 70%. It's one standard–100%. God doesn't grade on a curve. You either make 100% or you have failed (James 2:10). No man can make 100%, that's why Jesus (God) came to earth and became a man to pay for all our shortcomings.** He did it to fulfill the law, thereby making 100% for us because we couldn't; and He did it to deposit it into our individual account available by ONLY believing and putting faith in Him.

Since believing in Jesus is the only way into relationship, salvation, and right standing with God, every person can make it; good or bad, better or worse, 99.99% or 85%, if they only **believe** in Jesus as their Lord and Savior (Romans 10:9-10).

Christianity is not a list of do's and don'ts like all other religions. Believing in Jesus is the greatest equalizer of those who are not as good as others. Bad and good, we can all choose to believe regardless of how good our works and performance are.

The way to receive salvation is **ONLY by faith** not by works, good deeds, and good performance. Faith in Jesus is the only requirement for salvation (John 6:28-29; Acts 16:30-33, Mark 16:1; John 1:12, 3:15-16, 36, 20:31, Romans 5:1-2, 10:9-10, Galatians 3:22, 26, Ephesians 2:8-9; Romans 3:20-31). **Faith in Jesus and His finished work at the cross is the ONLY requirement for salvation and the only thing we can do to receive salvation.**

Although our actions are important, they do not produce salvation, right standing with God, and relationship with God. Our performances or actions are not the **root** of our salvation and right standing with God, but just the **fruit** of that relationship. All religions teach the very opposite of this. **We cannot work or perform our way into heaven. We can only believe our way into it.** Christianity is a relationship with God, not a set of rules.

Below are some scriptures that teach faith as the only requirement for salvation.

a) *"For if Abraham were justified by works, he hath whereof to glory; but not before God. For what saith the Scripture? Abraham believed God, and it was counted unto him for righteousness. Now to him that worketh is the reward not reckoned of grace, but of debt. But to him that worketh not, but believeth on him that justifieth the ungodly, his faith is counted for righteousness."* –Romans 4:2-5

    i) Abraham did not work for God to become righteous. He believed God and was declared righteous.

    ii) To be justified, to be made righteous with God, to be born again, to come into relationship with God through Jesus, you must only believe and work (perform) not.

b) *"But as many as received him, to them gave he power to become the sons of God, even to them that believe on his name." –*John1:12

    i) All who believe or believed in Christ Jesus have been given the power to become the sons of God.

    ii) Notice it says those who "believe," not those who perform or work. Salvation (prosperity, healing, peace, deliverance, and wholeness) comes only by believing.

c) *"For God so loved the world, that he gave his only begotten Son, that whosoever believeth in him should not perish, but have everlasting life. For God sent not his Son into the world to condemn the world; but that the world through him might be saved." –*John 3:16-17

    i) This promise is to those who believe, in other words, believers. Salvation comes by believing, not doing. We are saved (born again) through faith in Jesus not through our works or performance. Circumcision, water baptism, tithing, giving alms, going to church, etc. do not produce salvation. We MUST believe in the Lord Jesus Christ.

d) *"He that believeth on the Son hath everlasting life: and he that believeth not the Son shall not see life; but the wrath of God abideth on him." –*John 3:36

    i) He that believes in the Son (Jesus) has everlasting life. It does not say he that works, keeps the law, and does all these good deeds. Again, good deeds and good works are important in this life but not for the purpose of salvation or relationship with God. It takes only **believing** to enter into relationship with God and receive salvation.

e) *"Then said they unto him, what shall we do, that we might work the works of God? Jesus answered and said unto them, this is the work of God, that ye believe on him whom he hath sent." –*John 6:28-29

i) These men sincerely wanted to know what they could DO to be saved. This verse revealed to them what they had to DO. It was to believe on Him. That's the work that one should do.

ii) According to Colossians 2:6, we received Jesus by faith, and we continue to walk with Him and receive from Him by faith.

f) *"But these are written, that ye might believe that Jesus is the Christ, the Son of God; and that believing ye might have life through his name."* –John 20:31

i) Believing in Jesus produces life. Like previous verses, this verse talks about only believing, not performing or our good works and deeds.

g) *"Neither is there salvation in any other: for there is none other name under heaven given among men, whereby we must be saved."* –Acts 4:12

i) Salvation comes only by faith in the name of Jesus, not in the name of Buddha, Krishna, Mohammed, and so forth.

h) *"Therefore, by the deeds of the law there shall no flesh be justified in his sight: for by the law is the knowledge of sin. But now the righteousness of God without the law is manifested, being witnessed by the law and the prophets; Even the righteousness of God which is by faith of Jesus Christ unto all and upon all them that believe: for there is no difference: For all have sinned, and come short of the glory of God; Being justified freely by his grace through the redemption that is in Christ Jesus: Whom God hath set forth to be a propitiation through faith in his blood, to declare his righteousness for the remission of sins that are past, through the forbearance of God; To declare, I say, at this time his righteousness: that he might be just, and the justifier of him which believeth in Jesus."* –Romans 3:20-26

i) There is no good act or work that can make any man righteous before God. If our performance could justify us, there would be no need for Jesus. Jesus came because our deeds, actions, and performances could not produce the righteousness of God.

ii) The righteousness of God comes by faith in Jesus to all that believe.

i) *"Therefore, being justified by faith, we have peace with God through our Lord Jesus Christ." –Romans 5:1*

    i) We are justified by faith–not by the law, works, or performance.

j) *"That if thou shalt confess with thy mouth the Lord Jesus, and shalt believe in thine heart that God hath raised him from the dead, thou shalt be saved. For with the heart man believeth unto righteousness; and with the mouth confession is made unto salvation." –Romans 10:9-10*

    i) Notice this says believe in your heart, not work. Righteousness comes by believing not by working, keeping the law or performing.

k) *"But that no man is justified by the law in the sight of God, it is evident: for, The just shall live by faith." –Galatians 3:11*

    i) This verse says that **NO MAN** is justified or made righteous by the law (works, their good deeds, performance) in the sight of God.

l) *"But the Scripture hath concluded all under sin, that the promise by faith of Jesus Christ might be given to them that believe. For ye are all the children of God by faith in Christ Jesus." –Galatians 3:22, 26*

    i) The promise is for them that believe, not them that work.

    ii) We become children of God by faith in the Lord Jesus Christ.

m) *"For by grace are ye saved through faith; and that not of yourselves: it is the gift of God: Not of works, lest any man should boast." –Ephesians 2:8-9*

    i) Salvation is received not by works. It's not by performance. No one can boast. It's by grace through faith. We put faith in God's grace (Jesus and His finished work on the cross)

n) *"And brought them out, and said, Sirs, what must I do to be saved? And they said, Believe on the Lord Jesus Christ, and thou shalt be saved, and thy house.*

And they spake unto him the word of the Lord, and to all that were in his house." –Act 16:30-32

i) When these men asked how to be saved, Paul's answer to them further verifies what I have been saying in this teaching. He did not say be good, do good, keep the law, do good works and deeds and so forth. He said, **"Believe on the Lord Jesus Christ and thou shalt be saved."**

ii) We learn that the Bible teaches that it took only faith in the Lord Jesus to be saved–period. Nothing more to it and nothing less! So, when these men believed on the Lord, they were then baptized in water.

The Word of God doesn't say, "whosoever obeys Him perfectly", it doesn't say, "whoever never fails again", and it certainly doesn't say "whoever keeps all His commandments". It simply says, "whoever **believes** in Him". Whoever believes in Him will not perish but have eternal life. **The only action needed on your part is to believe and receive.**

Chapter Six

Was Jesus God or a Man?

This is one of the most important questions I have ever dealt with in detail. In my book, *Jesus; God or Man?*, I deal with this subject in depth. Here is the attempt to answer this same question—I will briefly show you some of the basic principles that I believe will be helpful in answering this question.

"Jesus—God or man?" is a question that almost everyone has thought of at some point, Christian or non-Christian. It's a question worth much consideration and discussion. Let's take a deep journey through the Scriptures, examining what they have to say about Jesus. Was He truly God or was He truly man? Could He be both? Could He be 50% God and 50% man? Or could He be 100% God and 100% man? Which is it?

Jesus was not just a good man sent from God, or some kind of angel, a good master, a good teacher, and a good prophet. Jesus was and is God. This is the most important statement of the New Testament, and on this truth, hangs all other truths. Although most people do not pay attention to this truth, it is the most important truth the Bible presents. Many people say that Jesus was a good man. Although that is true, it's not the whole truth.

If Jesus was only a man, then regardless of how good He was, His life could only provide a substitute for one other man. But it's well established in Scripture that Jesus' death was the payment for the sins of the whole world (1 John 2:2).

This would have been impossible if Jesus was just a good man. He was not a mere man or else His sacrifice would not be worth the payment and substitution for all mankind.

If Jesus was just a man, then you are still in your sins, and no one can be saved. Of course, that is not true. It would make all life hopeless and meaningless had Jesus been only a man. If Jesus was only a man, then His sacrifice was worthless to the whole world.

God the Father did not send a man less than Himself to pay for the sins of the entire human race. No mere man would qualify, no not one. Then what made Jesus qualify? Well, Jesus was God the Son, and that, above all else, made the difference. If Jesus' sacrifice was a perfect, complete, and blameless sacrifice, then it could not have been lesser than what God the Father would offer Himself. It had to be equal. What Jesus offered is equal to what God the Father would have offered.

Since Jesus was God, His life was worth more than every human life since creation. Indeed, it was worth more than the sum of the universe that He created. Jesus made an overpayment for our sins. He paid what we owed and beyond! What a Savior! Let's assume you owed $10, 000 on your car. When Jesus decided to pay for it on your behalf, He paid a billion dollars. He paid more than enough.

Just believing that Jesus was another good man, a teacher but not God, is neither the Gospel of Jesus nor the doctrine of Christ. It falls short of God's standard and expectation of your faith in Him, and that belief alone would not make Him the better sacrifice for you and would lead you into a search for more. Yet, there is nothing more. Jesus is all of it.

If all that God needed was just a good man to die for the sins of the entire world, then none would try to compete against Jesus. The truth is, God wasn't looking for just a good man to do this. He knew He was going to do this Himself because He was the only one capable, and He did it when he became a man named Jesus. Jesus *was* God incarnate. God needed **God** to die to reconcile man back to Himself, and that left only God–Jesus in the qualification race. No man would qualify beyond merely being good, which none is.

Jesus was His own class. Although this God-Man, Jesus, came dressed in a physical body, He was not merely another man like you and me. He was God manifest in the flesh–God incarnate (1 Tim. 3:16). Jesus humbled Himself and took upon Himself the form of a servant (Phil. 2:7). This is one of the greatest truths in the Bible: Almighty God came to Earth in human form.

Now that being said, we must not let the physical body of Jesus blind us to who He was and the fact that God became our friend. It's important to know that Jesus was and is God because only then can you have true relationship with Him. I believe ignorance of this truth would mean you are having relationship with someone other than God or lesser than God–hence no salvation and eternal life.

Equal with God

"And therefore did the Jews persecute Jesus, and sought to slay him, because he had done these things on the Sabbath day. But Jesus answered them, My Father worketh hitherto, and I work. Therefore the Jews <u>sought the more</u> to kill him, because he not only had broken the Sabbath, but said also that God was his Father, making himself equal with God."

–John 5:16-18 *(Underlined mine).*

An examination of this verse speaks volumes on how the Jews and others understood what it meant for Jesus to call God His Father. All through Jesus' ministry and life, He addressed God as Father. As New Testament believers, we can now call God our Father as Matthew 6:9 teaches. This privilege was purchased for us by our union with and faith in Jesus as our Lord and Savior. However, it does not bestow divinity upon us.

Note that there were two reasons–Healing on Sabbath and calling God His Father–why the Jews wanted to kill Jesus. But of those two reasons, the most outstanding was that Jesus said that "God was His Father", making Himself equal with God. They were most upset that Jesus had called God His Father.

Wait a minute. What was wrong with Jesus calling God His Father? The Jews understood that Jesus, by calling God His Father, was making Himself equal to God. It wasn't a question of "how can God have a son"; it was about Jesus making Himself equal with God. You see, it was obvious that no one had to tell them at this point what it meant. They already knew it. It's like they were studying or had learned this truth, which actually verifies and attests to Jesus' claim.

I think their reasoning about Jesus was true. Jesus was making Himself equal with God because He was equal with God (Phil. 2:6). He was God. He was equal with God the Father, and these people should not have sought to kill Him because He was speaking the truth. Jesus wouldn't have called God His Father if He wasn't equal to Him. They were blinded by the humanity of Jesus (His physical body), but they understood what it meant to call God His Father. I have spoken to hundreds of people about this striking truth, and it's like a light turned on inside of them. It clicked. And I pray that you will not be an exception.

The Rich, Young Ruler

Mark 10:17-20 talks about a rich, young ruler who came running to Jesus, knelt down, and asked Him, *"Good Master, what shall I do that I may inherit eternal life?"*

Publicly, this young man looked good, but his heart held something different. He looked good as he ran and knelt before Jesus. Jesus was God and was able to look beyond this man's outward display straight to his heart (1 Sam. 16:7). As He looked in his heart, He knew that this man wasn't willing to elevate Him to His rightful place as God. The young ruler's heart wasn't right, neither was his question. Because he believed he had kept all the commandments, which wasn't even true, he asked Jesus, "Good Master, what shall I do to inherit eternal life?" He believed that eternal life had to be earned. He thought he had to perform or do certain things to produce, earn, or receive eternal life.

You can't earn your way to God. No way, Jose! It's not what we do for God that produces eternal life (a relationship with God the Father through Jesus), but what Jesus has done for us. Eternal life is a gift to be received, not a wage to be earned (Eph.2:8-9; Rom. 10:9-10; Mk. 16:16; John 1:12; Acts 16:30-31). This man was trying to earn eternal life. Not good, and definitely not smart!

In Mark 10, verse 18, Jesus asks him, *"...Why callest me good? There is none good but one, that is, God."* In other words, Jesus was saying, either call me God, since you said I am good, or don't call me good. Jesus was saying that God alone is good, and if you recognize that I am good, why don't you call me God? After all, I am. The young man recognized Jesus just as a good man, but not as God, just as many people today believe that he was just a good man, an angel, or a second-place god. Jesus wanted to get him to put total faith in Him, not just a partial faith.

My friend, just as we see in this passage, calling Jesus a good man, a prophet, a teacher, or a leader is not enough. We must acknowledge and recognize Him as God. The young man needed to acknowledge Jesus as God, but Mark 10:20 shows that he didn't. No man can earn God's salvation. You can't live "good enough" to earn it. You can only get it as a gift–free. Once you try to earn it, it ceases to be a gift. And as a matter of fact, you can't earn it. It's just impossible.

"And he answered and said unto Him, Master..."–we see here that the young ruler dropped good from good Master, and he referred to Jesus just as Master. Remember, Jesus had told him to either call Him God or quit calling Him good. In Mark 10:18 and here in verse 20, he dropped the good and just called Jesus Master. Amazing! This reveals the heart of the young man and his religious displays of running and kneeling. He wasn't willing to worship Jesus as God.

Many people today are just like this rich, young ruler. They make all these religious displays, but in their hearts, Jesus is not given His rightful place. He is still a good master to some, and to others, He is master–but not God. Jesus desires you to relate to Him as He is–God. God is good. If Jesus is good, you might as well believe, and call Him who He truly is–God. **Jesus will not accept anything less than God** because He was and is God. I mean, why should He? He was God, and He is God. Amen!

This scripture reveals that Jesus was God and that people know it in their hearts but reject it. If Jesus is God, then you can be saved and have a personal relationship with Him, but if He is not God, then you are lost forever because you can't have a relationship with another human being that produces salvation and eternal life. Jesus is Lord and God. Hallelujah!

The Very Nature of God

"Who being in the form of God, thought it not robbery to be equal with God: but made himself of no reputation, and took upon Him the form of a servant, and was made in the likeness of men."

–Philippians 2:6-7

The word *"form"* is the word for *"nature."* The NIV says that Jesus was *"the very nature of God."* The Message Bible says, *"...he set aside the privileges of deity and took on the status of a slave, became human! Having become human, he stayed human."*

This scripture goes on to prove that Jesus was God and that He did not think it was robbery or unjust to be equal with God. Jesus was equal with God, and He knew it. He didn't think He was robbing or stealing from God by being equal with Him. Yet even with that level of knowledge, He said, "I will become a servant. I will limit and confine myself in a physical body." Amazing! Therefore, God became a man who was called Jesus.

Understanding that He was not in His full glory as God on earth because of the limitations of a physical body, Jesus had to depend on the Father for guidance, fellowship, and communion. They were united to the point that one could not operate independent of the other (See Gen. 1:26, *"Let Us make man in Our own image...."* [emphasis mine])

So, Jesus, in His all earthly ministry, had to depend on God the Father and the Holy Spirit (Acts 5:4), as we can also see in Acts 10:38. That explains why Jesus, who was God and man at the same time, had to pray to God the Father. He had limitations because He had a physical body and needed to depend on the Father, who had sent Him. For example, Jesus was God and man, yet He had to be physically taught how to speak, walk, dress, etc. He had to learn all the basic things that you and I have learned. He increased in favor and wisdom (Luke 2:52). Jesus emotionally and physically felt pain, intense pain; the cross wasn't some game that Jesus would just easily endure. All the sin of the entire human race was carried by Him. It was all placed on Him. It was such a painful experience that it can't be portrayed on TV and fully understood. It takes a revelation from the Holy Spirit. A movie could only do so much.

The Bible says that He became sin. "He that knew no sin, became sin that you might be made the righteousness of God" (2 Cor. 5:21). He took your sins and gave you His righteousness, benefits, and privileges. There was an exchange. He took all your mess and gave you His goodness. Today we are the righteousness of Jesus (God) because our righteousness comes from Him.

Finally, Jesus praying to the Father doesn't necessarily mean that He was petitioning God for something. Most people think prayer is nothing but petitioning (asking for something). Prayer is communion with God above all else. Sometimes this communion may involve asking or petitioning, but it doesn't always have to. You can pray without asking. It's probable that Jesus was praying, yet not asking.

What God the Father Says about Jesus…

It's one thing for me and for others to say Jesus was and is God, but it's an even greater testimony to see God the Father calling Jesus God! This is such a powerful ingredient to all we have seen because it continues to confirm the things I have said thus far in this book.

A close look at Hebrews 1:1-8 speaks volumes to the truth that Jesus was God. To start with, Hebrews 1:3 says, "Who being the brightness of his glory, and the express image of his person…". This scripture says that Jesus is the brightness of His (God the Father's) glory. Isaiah 42:8 says that the Lord will not share His glory with another. Therefore, Jesus is the Lord since He is the brightness of God the Father's glory. Jesus = Brightness of the Father's Glory. Romans 3:23 calls Jesus *the glory of God.* This is more proof of Jesus' deity.

Hebrews 1:3 continues to say that Jesus was the "express image" of God the Father. The term express image means an exact copy. Wow! Jesus was exactly like the Father. He was an exact copy. He perfectly represented God to us. If we look at Jesus, we are looking at God the Father (John 14:9). If you see Jesus, you don't need to still try to see the Father. You have already seen Him. Now, some might be thinking of the physical part of Jesus, but we need to think about His Spirit. In His Spirit, He was an exact copy of God the Father, and His works and actions here on earth were a perfect picture and representation of the Father.

Hebrews 1:6 goes on to say "…and let the angels of God worship him." God commanded all the angels to worship Jesus. Notice that not just a few of the angels, but all the angels. So, if all worship is reserved for God alone (Isa. 42:8), why would God the Father command all the angels to worship Jesus if He was not God or was inferior? It's clear that God the Father knew that Jesus was who He claimed to be and so commanded the angels to worship Him. There is no one in the Scriptures that God ever commanded to be worshipped, except Jesus–God the Son. This proves that Jesus was God and deserved worship (Psa. 45:11, 95:6).

God would not have all the angels worship someone inferior to Him. The person that God commands to be worshipped has to be God or equal to Him. Jesus was equal to God. He wasn't inferior. He was God in a physical body, and He deserved worship, even by all the angels, just as the Father. Let me also say that the angels would not have worshipped an equal, only one who was greater. Jesus was greater–indeed, far greater.

Thy Throne, O God

"But unto the Son he (God the Father) saith, thy throne, O God is forever and ever: a sceptre of righteousness, is the sceptre of thy kingdom."

–Hebrews 1:8 *(parentheses mine)*

I love this scripture. It speaks volumes. God the Father is referring to Jesus as God. This is more conclusive proof of the deity of the Lord Jesus Christ. It is proof that Jesus was and is God, not a god, but GOD.

Wait a minute. God called Jesus God. Selah. Why? It's only because Jesus was and is God. God would not have called Jesus God if He wasn't God. This would have been a complete lie. It is well established in Scripture that God cannot lie–FULLSTOP. Well, I'm glad He called Jesus God because this is the greatest proof, above all the others I've been pouring out so far. Jesus was and still is God, not just a mere man.

After God the Father commanded all the angels to worship Jesus, He went on to call Jesus God. This is a truth that cannot be ignored. It's pivotal. Hallelujah! Jesus was God. Jesus is Lord God Almighty. He also said that His throne is **forever and ever**. In other words, only the throne of God is everlasting. God's throne is forever and ever.

Wonderful, Counselor, The mighty God, The everlasting Father, the prince of peace

"For unto us a child is born, unto us a Son is given; and the government shall be upon his shoulder and his name shall be called Wonderful, Counselor, The mighty God, The everlasting Father, the prince of peace."

–Isaiah 9:6

This is one of the most powerful scriptures in the Old Testament. God spoke through the prophet Isaiah what was going to happen in the future. Jesus was to be born to us, and His name was to be Wonderful, Counselor, the mighty God, the everlasting Father, the prince of peace. God, through the prophet Isaiah, called Jesus "the mighty God." The word "the" is a definite article. It is referring to "only one person," excluding anyone else. It is clear that this is speaking about one person. If God the Father is the mighty God, Jesus is equally the mighty God. Furthermore, God continued on to call Jesus "The everlasting Father." This proves the point that Jesus was and is equal to the Father and that they are one (John 5:18; 10:30). It also further verifies the truth that when we see Jesus, we have seen the Father (John 14:9).

God with Us

"Behold, a virgin shall be with child, and shall bring forth a son, and they shall call his name Emmanuel, which being interpreted is, God with us."

–Matthew 1:23

During the Christmas season, we tend to read this passage often, right? Right. Have you ever stopped and thought about what the name Emmanuel means, and why Jesus was to be called Emmanuel?

It's important to understand why Jesus was to be called Emmanuel. Why not some other name? The meaning of that name is very significant. It means "God with Us". Jesus was God who came to be with us, and his name Emmanuel was saying the very same thing. Way before Jesus was born, the instruction to His parents was to call Him Emmanuel, which means "God with Us". Surely, Jesus was God with Us. Yes, God. Even at birth, Jesus was God. This passage helps continue to build the case that Jesus was and is God. Indeed, God came to be with us.

Jesus and the Father Are One

"I and my father are one."

–John 10:30

Jesus had already received a violent response from the people–the Jews, the scribes, and the Pharisees, when He called God His Father (John 5:17-18). They understood that as Him claiming deity. Yet in this verse, He not only calls God His Father but says that He and the Father are one. The word one in this passage is not the regular "one" we commonly use. It means more than singleness of purpose. It denotes a single one to the exclusion of another. Jesus and the Father are ONE. Note that this was the second time that Jesus claimed deity, and the Jews wanted to stone Him after His statements made in verses 29 through 38. If they had understood His statements to mean that He wasn't proclaiming His deity, then they would have left Him alone.

Ye Shall Die in Your Sins... I Am He

"I said therefore unto you, that ye shall die in your sins: for if ye believe not that I am he, ye shall die in your sins."

–John 8:24

Here Jesus proclaims Himself as the *"I am."* In Exodus 3:14 when God revealed Himself to Moses, He proclaimed and identified Himself as "I am."

God the Father calls Himself "I am" (Ex. 3:14), and Jesus calls Himself "I am" three times (John 8:24, 8:28, 8:58). Jesus was the *"Great I am"* of Exodus 3:14, manifest in the flesh (1 Tim. 3:16).

Also, right before His crucifixion in the garden of Gethsemane, Jesus said, *"I am"* and just that statement knocked the 600 men who came to arrest Him backwards to the ground. There was tremendous power in the words "I am", just as when it was spoken to Moses (Ex. 3:14). Another important part of John 8:24 is that it says, *"If ye believe not that I am he, ye shall die in your sins."*

This verse is saying that failure to believe and acknowledge that Jesus is the "I AM" (God) (Ex. 3:14), means you can't be saved and shall die in your sins. Why? Because Jesus was God, and if He wasn't, then you will die in your sins, and all mankind is doomed. Hallelujah! Since He was God, there is hope for mankind. Man can be saved through faith in Jesus Christ.

If we do not believe that Jesus was God, then we can't be saved. Jesus in His humanity alone could not save the world. It would be impossible because He had to be God. If we believe in a "Jesus" lesser than God, we can't truly be saved. Jesus = God. We can't have a relationship with God without receiving Jesus. Jesus was God, and that invites us into a relationship with God the Father. Jesus was and is God with us—Emmanuel.

I Am the Way, the Truth and the Life

"Jesus saith unto him, I am the way, the truth, and the life: no man cometh unto the Father, but by me."

–John 14:6

Jesus did not say He was **a** way, **a** truth and **a** life. No! He claimed to be **the** Way, **the** Truth and **the** Life. Again, the word "the" is a definite article. This leaves no room for other means of salvation. This statement leaves no alternatives. Any religion that doesn't acknowledge Jesus as the ONLY way of salvation is in error and false.

Jesus is not just the way...FULL STOP. He is also the truth and the life. If Jesus is not the LORD of your life, you have missed the truth. Jesus = Truth. Notice also that it says, "NO man comes to the Father except through Jesus." If Jesus is not the Lord of your life, you have missed God. I don't care if you say you "believe in God." If you reject Jesus, you have rejected the True Life. Jesus = Life. No Jesus, no life.

Believe the Works

"But if I do, though ye believe not me, believe the works: that ye may know, and believe, that the Father is in me, and I in him."

–John 10:38

Miracles are great witnesses to the power of God, and here, Jesus tells the Jews to at least believe the miracles, signs, and wonders He did. Then they would know that He is God (one with the Father) and that the Father is in Him, and He is in the Father. He was saying that considering the signs and wonders would open their hearts to believe in who He had said He was, "I and the Father are one" (John 10:30). The Father is in Jesus, and Jesus is in Him. This is expressing a great degree of unity. I can't find any other words to explain it. John 10:30 sums it up.

Ye Say Well

"Ye call me Master and Lord: and ye say well; for so I am. If I then, your Lord and Master, have washed your feet; ye also ought to wash one another's feet."

–John 13:13-14

In this passage of scripture, Jesus said that His disciples called Him Lord. He went on to say that they were right to call Him Lord because He was. Deuteronomy 6:4 says, "The Lord our God is one Lord." Jesus is Lord. Jesus was and still is God.

Think about this for a moment. If Jesus was not LORD, He would not have commended the disciples for calling Him LORD. He would have rebuked it.

Honoring the Son = Honoring the Father

"That all men should honour the Son, even as they honour the Father. He that honoureth not the Son honoureth not the Father which hath sent him."

–John 5:23

This is one of the strongest arguments of a well-established truth in Scripture: Jesus was and truly is God. We can't just honor Jesus, but we have to honor Him even as (in like manner or the same way) we honor the Father. If you do not honor Jesus, you have not honored the Father. There is no way around this. You can't dishonor the LORD in an effort to honor the Father. As a matter of fact, you can't even know the Father without Jesus because Jesus reveals the Father to us all.

This is what draws a line and separates true Christianity from the religions of the world. Most religions honor Jesus as a great man (examples: Jehovah's Witnesses, Islam, and the Unification Church, etc.) but are violently opposed to making Jesus equal to the Almighty God (1 John 2:23). This scripture also says **all men**, not just a few but all. If you are a human being, this scripture applies to you. It's speaking to you.

Knowing Jesus = Knowing the Father

"Then said they unto him, Where is thy Father? Jesus answered, Ye neither know me, nor my Father: if ye had known me, ye should have known my Father also."

–John 8:19

Here, we see Jesus calling God His Father. John 5:18 verifies that Jesus was equal to God the Father. That's why He called Him "my father". Jesus also said that if they had known Him, they would have known the Father as well. Knowing Jesus is knowing the Father. This establishes that Jesus was God and that Jesus, and the Father are ONE, just as John 10:30 says. This is saying that a person who doesn't know (have personal relationship with) Jesus, doesn't know the Father.

Anyone who says that you can have a relationship with God the Father without first believing on God the Son, Jesus Christ, such as Jehovah's Witnesses, the Unification Church, Mormons, Jesuits, the Unity Church, Islam and many others, is teaching error and has the spirit of anti-Christ (1 John 4:3; 2 John 7-9).

Jesus is **the way** to the Father, not "a way." There is no short cut. If you don't believe and receive Jesus as your Lord and Savior, you cannot claim to have or know the Father. If you let Jesus in, the Father comes in along with Him, but you can't let the Father in without letting in Jesus.

"If ye had known me, ye should have known my Father also: and from henceforth ye know him, and have seen him."

–John 14:7

This verse also clearly shows that knowing Jesus is knowing the Father. This is not only because Jesus did what He saw the Father do, but because He was God in the flesh–God with us. Knowing Jesus equates to knowing the Father because they are one, but you can't know the Father without knowing Jesus first. In other words, relationship starts with Jesus before it goes to the Father. Anyone who tries bypassing Jesus is joking. If you know Jesus, you will know the Father. Until you are in a relationship with Jesus, you can't have a relationship with God the Father. Jesus is the door to relationship with the Father.

Again, Knowing Jesus = Knowing the Father. However, knowing the Father does not equal knowing Jesus because you can't know the Father unless you first know Jesus.

Receiving Jesus = Receiving God the Father

"…he that receiveth me receiveth him that sent me."

–John 13:20

This is another powerful passage in line with all my other statements. Here, Jesus continues to emphasize that receiving Him is receiving God the Father who sent Him. Jesus was equal to the Father (John 10:30). Receiving Him is equivalent to receiving the Father because they are one (John 10:30, 14:6-7).

Denying Jesus is denying God. Acknowledging Jesus is acknowledging God (1 John 2:23). Hating Jesus is hating God (John 15:23). Honoring Jesus is honoring God (John 5:23) because Jesus is God and is equal to God the Father.

Hating Jesus = Hating God the Father

"He that hateth me hateth my Father also."

–John 15:23

Oh boy, this is a powerful verse! How many religions or people hate Jesus, yet claim to be in relationship with God? This is one more verse in a list of scriptures in which Jesus equated any form of rejection of Him, or who He claimed, as rejection of God the Father.

Say it like this: Rejecting or Hating Jesus = Rejecting or Hating the Father. Any group or religion that claims to have access to God the Father without exalting Jesus to an equal position is completely deceived. Hating Jesus is hating God because Jesus is God and equal to the Father (John 10:30; Phil. 2:6).

Four Facts of Jesus' Deity

Fact 1: Worship

Worship is an attribute reserved for God alone.

Here are eleven instances where Jesus was worshipped. Eight of them are mentioned by Matthew, Mark, Luke and John. (Matt. 2:2; 2:11; 8:2; 9:18; 14:33; 15:25; 20:20; 28:9, 17; Mark 5:6; Luke 24:52; John 9:38). The fact that Jesus received the worship of these people further attests to the fact that He was God manifest in the flesh (1 Tim. 3:16). He was and is God.

Fact 2: Forgiveness of Sins

Just like worship, forgiveness of sins is an attribute reserved for God alone.

"When Jesus saw their faith, he said unto the sick of the palsy, Son, thy sins be forgiven thee. But there were certain of the scribes sitting there, and

reasoning in their hearts, why doth this man speak blasphemies? Who can forgive sins but God only?"

–Mark 2:5-7

Fact 3: Creation

Just like worship and forgiving sins, this is another attribute reserved for God alone.

"In whom we have redemption through his blood, even the forgiveness of sins: Who is the image of the invisible God, the firstborn of every creature: For by him were all things created, that are in heaven, and that are in earth, visible and invisible, whether they be thrones, or dominions, or principalities, or powers: all things were created by him, and for him: And he is before all things, and by him all things consist."

–Colossians 1:14-17

"Hast thou not known? hast thou not heard that the everlasting God, the LORD, the Creator of the ends of the earth, fainteth not, neither is weary? there is no searching of his understanding."

–Isaiah 40:28

Fact 4: Savior

A close study of Scripture clearly reveals that Jesus is the Savior of mankind. Many times, you will find Jesus being referred to as the Savior.

"And my spirit hath rejoiced in God my savior."

–Luke 1:47

God is called the Savior. Mary rejoiced in God, her Savior. Of whom was she speaking? She was speaking of Jesus, her Savior and God. She said God was her Savior. So, just like Mary did, we can clearly see that God is our Savior. "For unto you is born this day in the city of David a Savior, which is Christ the Lord." (Luke 2:11).

Chapter Seven

Since Jesus Had a Physical Body, Did He Sin? So, If Jesus Was God, How Could He Pray to God? Was Jesus Praying to Himself?

The sinlessness of Jesus is a vital Christian doctrine. It is foundational to Christianity because if Jesus had been a sinner Himself, then He too would have needed a savior. He certainly couldn't have been anyone else's Savior. But Jesus was so pure that even His enemies attested to His innocence and purity.

Here is what the Word of God teaches about the sinlessness of Jesus:

a) *"Which of you convinceth me of sin? And if I say the truth, why do ye not believe me?"* –John 8:46

Raise your hand if you would make such a statement. If you raised your hand, you are a hypocrite! You are a liar. No one can stand and say they have no sin. The only exception was and is Jesus. The Bible says that "all have sinned and come short of the glory of God" (Rom. 3:23). Jesus was the only exception to this truth because He was not just a man. He was more than a man. He was God-Man. He was God in a physical body. That's why He asked these Jews a question they could not answer. Jesus had no sin in His life that these people could point out. If Jesus had committed even one single sin, this mob would have spoken up. He had none, and these Jews knew it.

No one among this mob could find any sin in Jesus' life. If they would have had any indictment against Jesus, they certainly would have spoken up in response to Jesus' question. But God's Word says that "all have sinned and come short of the glory of God" (Rom. 3:23). The "all" this verse speaks about is *all men*, but even though Jesus was a man, this verse does not include Him because He never sinned—thus this question, "Which of you convinceth me of sin?"

A comparison of these two scriptures reveals that Jesus did not sin. God cannot sin. Because Jesus was God in the flesh (1 Tim. 3:16), He never sinned (2 Cor. 5:21; Heb. 4:15, 7:26). 1 Peter 2:22 says that Jesus did not sin. Although Pilate was not a godly man, he willfully said he had found no fault in this man, Jesus (Luke 23:4, 14-22; Matt. 27:19).

b) *"Who did no sin, neither was guile found in his mouth."* –1 Peter 2:22

Here is yet another scripture attesting to the fact that Jesus never sinned. What a testimony of His divinity. He never spoke in deceit. He committed no sin. How much clearer can that get? This is a vital issue. If Jesus was a sinner, then His life was not holy enough to atone for the whole human race. But if He was the sinless Son of God, then His life was worth more than **all** of humanity. This also testifies of His deity. Surely, Jesus was God.

c) *"And he made his grave with the wicked, and with the rich in his death; because he had done no violence, neither was any deceit in his mouth."* –Isaiah 53:9

This prophecy was about Jesus. Years before Jesus came on the scene, the prophet Isaiah prophesied, and the Scriptures show that Jesus did no violence and spoke no deceit. In other words, He never committed sin.

d) *"For we have not a high priest which cannot be touched with the feeling of our infirmities; but was in all points tempted like as were, yet without sin."* –Hebrews 4:15.

This verse clearly states that although Jesus became like one of us and was tempted (Matt. 4:1-4) like all of us, He was still without sin.

e) *"For such an high priest became us, who is holy, harmless, undefiled, separate from sinners, and made higher than the heavens."* –Hebrews 7:26

All of these qualities of Jesus were mentioned in comparison to the Old Testament priests. They had to be holy, harmless, undefiled, and separate from sinners. Jesus was all of these things in a way that no sinful man could ever be. Plus, He was not only exalted in the eyes of men as the high priest was, but He was exalted to sit at the right hand of God–as God. Jesus was better in every way.

What a paradox and a necessity that we, who were unholy, harmful, defiled, and companions of sinners, would have Jesus be our High Priest, ever living to intercede for us. No one has ever been able to point out a single sin Jesus committed because He never committed any. He broke some of the Jewish traditions and interpretations of the Law, like the Sabbath, but He wasn't in error. Their interpretations were in error.

Even though Jesus had a physical body, He sinned not. Had He sinned, He would have been disqualified from being the Savior of the world. However, Scripture has it clearly spelled out that Jesus sinned not.

So, If Jesus Was God, How Could He Pray to God? Was Jesus Praying to Himself?

Jesus was no less than God on earth, praying to the Father.

It's important to understand that Jesus, as God on earth, praying to God the Father in heaven, demonstrates a unity between the two. The eternal Father and the eternal Son had an eternal relationship before Jesus took upon Himself the form of a man. And that exclusive unity between them never ceased when He came to the earth. Jesus did not become God the Son when He was born in Bethlehem. He has always been the Son of God from eternity past, still is God the Son, and always will be. As a matter of fact, in Luke 2:11, the angel called Jesus "Savior, Christ the Lord." That clearly shows that even at birth Jesus was Lord–God.

Jesus, God the Father, and the Holy Spirit have always existed, not as three Gods, but one God, existing or expressed in three persons. That's why Jesus claimed deity–because He was God (John 10:30). The Father, the Son, and the Holy Spirit are three co-equal persons existing as God–singular.

All that being said, it's important to remember that although Jesus was God, He was a man. Let me put it this way; He was God–Man. Jesus was so human that people struggled to accept that He was God. They looked at Him and saw nothing physically special. Isaiah 53:2 says that "… he hath no form nor comeliness; and when we shall see him, there is no beauty that we should desire him."

He wasn't one of those "beautiful people." This doesn't necessarily mean He was ugly, but He definitely wasn't physically special. Physically, He wasn't one of those handsome, flashy, six-pack-ab people everyone admires, wants to be around and be seen with, and receive recognition from. He was just plain and ordinary. If you had seen Him walk the earth, you wouldn't have been so impressed. There was nothing physically special about Him.

Jesus walked, ate, laughed, went to the bathroom, got dirty, got tired, slept, got angry, got hungry, and on and on the list goes. Jesus became like we are. Seeing all this about Jesus made it hard to believe this was God! Why? Because He looked so human that His physical being blinded some men to His spiritual being. The Spirit of Jesus was wall to wall God. On the *spiritual level*, Jesus was God, and on the *physical level*, He was a man. He was 100% God and 100% man. He wasn't 50/50.

Prior to becoming a man, Jesus, who was Almighty God, full of glory and majesty and honor, laid aside His glory and became a man. He took upon Himself the form of a servant and was made in the likeness of men. Jesus was still God when He became a man. Yet He concealed His divinity in a physical body. Thereby, the King became a servant!

Therefore, Jesus prayed to God the Father because the human part of Him (Jesus) who was subject to the Father, was and needed to be dependent on God the Father.

Chapter Eight

I'm a Giver, Why Is It That I'm Struggling Financially?

Giving is a biblical principle and there are many promises from God's Word to those who are givers. Unfortunately, many people think that all there is to prosper financially is giving, PERIOD. There is a lot more to it than just giving. If all it took is giving, then many people would be rich and financially prosperous. There is much more to giving than the gift.

The fact that some people are givers and yet still struggle financially is reason to prove that there is a lot more to prospering than just giving. Acts 20:35 says, *"It is more blessed to give than to receive."*

The Key Factors in Understanding Giving

A. Motives

The motivation of the gift or why we give is more important than the gift itself. If prosperity and financial increase were just about giving only, then pretty much everyone would be financially prosperous. However, there is much more to giving than the gift. We must have the right motivation whenever we give, otherwise, our gift will profit us nothing.

a) **Love**

The number one motive with which to give should be love. If we do not give with a motivation of love, we have just lost our gift. There is no harvest on such a gift. We should endeavor that whenever we give, we are driven by love.

   i)   *"And though I bestow all my goods to feed the poor, and though I give my body to be burned, and have not charity, it profiteth me nothing."*
       –1 Corinthians 13:3

b) To be seen of men

"Take heed that ye do not your alms before men, to be seen of them: otherwise ye have no reward of your Father which is in heaven. Therefore when thou doest thine alms, do not sound a trumpet before thee, as the hypocrites do in the synagogues and in the streets, that they may have glory of men. Verily I say unto you, they have their reward. But when thou doest alms, let not thy left hand know what thy right hand doeth: 4 That thine alms may be in secret: and thy Father which seeth in secret himself shall reward thee openly."

       –Matthew 6:1-4

Giving to impress others is not a godly motivation and will yield no return.

c) Pressure and coercion

We should not give when we are pressured and coerced. This is the wrong time and motivation to give. We have to be cheerful at heart when we give, or we have given for the wrong reason and this means no return.

   i)   *"Every man according as he purposeth in his heart, so let him give; not grudgingly, or of necessity: for God loveth a cheerful giver."*
       –2 Corinthians 9:7

d) Fear

Once fear is the reason we give to others or any cause, we have lost our money. We should never give when we are motivated by fear. Fear is a red flag for us not to give, at least not at that time.

i) *"There is no fear in love; but perfect love casteth out fear: because fear hath torment. He that feareth is not made perfect in love."* −1 John 4:18

ii) *"For God hath not given us the spirit of fear; but of power, and of love, and of a sound mind."* −2 Timothy 1:7

e) **Condemnation**

If we are giving out of condemnation, this is also a wrong time and motivation to give.

i) *"And hereby we know that we are of the truth, and shall assure our hearts before him. For if our heart condemn us, God is greater than our heart, and knoweth all things."* −1 John 3:19-20

ii) *"There is therefore now no condemnation to them which are in Christ Jesus, who walk not after the flesh, but after the Spirit."* −Romans 8:1

f) **Manipulation or arm-twisting**

Some giving is nothing but manipulation. We must be careful not to give to such endeavors. Manipulation is deceptive. We should not use ungodly tools and means to get godly results.

i) *"I want each of you to take plenty of time to think it over, and make up your own mind what you will give. That will protect you against sob stories and **arm-twisting**. God loves it when the giver delights in the giving."* −2 Corinthians 9:7

g) **Begging and pleading**

We should not give when we are begged and pleaded with. Pity is not the right motivation to give but compassion is. It is manipulation to play on people's emotions so as to cause them to give.

B. Ground

Giving is an investment in success. You can give to partake in one's success. Find good ground and invest in it. We must identify good ground and sow in it. Never give to a dead church that is not teaching the true Gospel or Word of God. If you do, you are subsidizing, promoting, and supporting what they are doing. If you don't give to them, they will either have to change what they preach or go out of "business". Not all soils are the same. The soil for rice is not the soil for apples or pineapples and so forth.

We should not just give anyhow or anywhere. Treat your giving as an investment that must go into a profitable business venture that will yield a return. If we would not invest in a dead business or one on life support, we should not give to dead ministries or preachers. Although there is a time to give to a need, it should not be the only way or reason we give.

Example of good ground found in scriptures:

a) Jesus

Luke 8:3 says, *"And Joanna the wife of Chuza Herod's steward, and Susanna, and many others, which ministered unto him of their substance."*

b) Paul

Philippians 4:15 says, *"Now ye Philippians know also, that in the beginning of the gospel, when I departed from Macedonia, no church communicated with me as concerning giving and receiving, but ye only."*

c) Elijah

1 Kings 17:9 says, *"Arise, get thee to Zarephath, which belongeth to Zidon, and dwell there: behold, I have commanded a widow woman there to sustain thee."*

d) Elisha

> 2 Kings 4:13 says, *"And he said unto him, Say now unto her, Behold, thou hast been careful for us with all this care; what is to be done for thee? wouldest thou be spoken for to the king, or to the captain of the host? And she answered, I dwell among mine own people."*

You must give where you are fed. If you eat at Andy's, pay at Andy's not a Rich's. All food from all restaurants doesn't taste the same, nor is it all good food. Pay and sow in good ground.

C. To whom are we giving?

We naturally expect a reward from whosoever we give to. If we are giving to man, then we should expect our reward from man but if we are giving to God, then our reward will come from the Lord. When you give, who are you giving to? Giving to the wrong person could hamper your financial increase.

D. Faithfulness and consistency in giving

Are you a seasonal giver or a consistent giver? One of the reasons we never receive is because we only give when it is convenient. It is like a farmer who plants seed only when he wants to or feels like it. Such a farmer will not abound with a huge crop come the time of harvest.

a) Giving should not be done whenever we feel like it. We have to develop an attitude to give whenever we are given opportunity because it's to our benefit. We should give whenever we have opportunity to give. The more seed you have in the ground, the more chances of a greater harvest.

   i) *"Honour the LORD with thy substance, and with the firstfruits of all thine increase: So shall thy barns be filled with plenty, and thy presses shall burst out with new wine."* –Proverbs 3:9-10

   ii) *"Now ye Philippians know also, that in the beginning of the gospel, when I departed from Macedonia, no church communicated with me as concerning giving and receiving, but ye only. For even in Thessalonica ye sent once and again unto my necessity. Not because I desire a gift: but I desire fruit that may abound to your account."* –Philippians 4:15-17

b) We should also sow during famine in faith. We can't hold back on planting. To reap, we must have sown (Galatians 6:7). Isaac (Genesis 26:12, 14 and 16) did this and got one hundred-fold the same year. God is not a respecter of persons (Romans 2:11), if He did it for Isaac, He will do the same for you, but you must sow.

We must consistently practice the principle of giving. You can't just pray, fast, cry, talk, or even anoint yourself into increase and abundance.

E. Work

Work is one of the dirtiest words to some people. They want to have money and financially prosper but they **will not work**. However, the Bible ties financial prosperity to work. God has placed a blessing in work. If we can get our hands to do something, prosperity and financial increase will be a result.

Money is the reward for solving problems. The more problems you solve, the more money you'll make. If you are broke and busted, it's because you aren't solving any problems or probably not enough of them.

It is interesting that God gave something to do (work) to a sinless man in the garden.

"Prayer is not in the success equation! Prayer is in the revelation equation. Success starts when you implement the instructions you receive in prayer."
                                        –Bishop Tudor Bismark.

Implementation of ideas separates those that have abundance and those in need. You can't live your life in your head dreaming. You must take action! Not next week, not tomorrow, but now.

a) *"The LORD shall command the blessing upon thee in thy **storehouses, and in all that thou settest thine hand unto**; and he shall bless thee in the land which the LORD thy God giveth thee."* –Deuteronomy 28:8

b) *"The LORD shall open unto thee his good treasure, the heaven to give the rain unto thy land in his season, and to bless all the work of thine hand: and thou shalt lend unto many nations, and thou shalt not borrow."* –Deuteronomy 28:12

c) *"But thou shalt remember the LORD thy God: for it is he that giveth thee power to get wealth, that he may establish his covenant which he swore unto thy fathers, as it is this day."* –Deuteronomy 8:18

d) *"And his master saw that the LORD was with him, and that the LORD made all that he did to prosper in his hand. The keeper of the prison looked not to anything that was **under his hand; because the LORD was with him, and that which he did**, the LORD made it to **prosper**."* –Genesis 39:3, 23

   i) Notice it says the Lord was with him (Joseph) *and* that which he did, and He made it prosper. In other words, if he did not do anything, he would miss out on the Lord being with him to prosper him.

e) *"…that the LORD thy **God may bless thee in all the work of thine hand which thou doest**."* –Deuteronomy 14:29

f) *"And the LORD thy **God will make thee plenteous in every work of thine hand**, in the fruit of thy body, and in the fruit of thy cattle, and in the fruit of thy land, for good: for the LORD will again rejoice over thee for good, as he rejoiced over thy fathers."* –Deuteronomy 30:9

g) Laziness

Lack and poverty are both married to laziness. One of the main reasons for lack and insufficiency is that many people are lazy. It is well known that the lazy and slothful aren't diligent and hardworking.

   i) *"The sluggard will not plow by reason of the cold; therefore, shall he beg in harvest, and have nothing."* –Proverbs 20:4

ii) *"He that tilleth his land shall have plenty of bread: but he that followeth after vain persons shall have poverty enough."* –Proverbs 28:19

iii) *"Go to the ant, thou sluggard; consider her ways, and be wise: Which having no guide, overseer, or ruler, Provideth her meat in the summer, and gathereth her food in the harvest. How long wilt thou sleep, O sluggard? when wilt thou arise out of thy sleep? Yet a little sleep, a little slumber, a little folding of the hands to sleep: So shall thy poverty come as one that traveleth, and thy want as an armed man."* –Proverbs 6:6-11

F. Cursing the little we have

One of the mistakes we make when we do not have enough is to curse what we have. Our attitude should be to bless the little you have and not curse it.

a) Jesus' example (Matthew 14:17-19) is the prime example. Here, with only five loaves and two fishes, considering the multitude He was about to feed, He could have cursed and complained over the little He had but He instead blessed it and it multiplied.

b) We should apply this same principle whenever we have little or not enough.

G. Poor stewardship and wasting

a) Pleasure and wine

i) *"He that loveth pleasure shall be a poor man: he that loveth wine and oil shall not be rich."* –Proverbs 21:17

b) Drunkard and glutton

i) *"For the drunkard and the glutton shall come to poverty: and drowsiness shall clothe a man with rags."* –Proverbs 23:21

c) Wrong company

i) *"Whoso loveth wisdom rejoiceth his father: but he that keepeth company with harlots spendeth his substance."* –Proverbs 29:3

H. Faith

Whenever we give, we must give in faith. If we give out of doubt, we will do without.

a) *"For verily I say unto you, That whosoever shall say unto this mountain, Be thou removed, and be thou cast into the sea; and shall not doubt in his heart, but shall believe that those things which he saith shall come to pass; he shall have whatsoever he saith."* –Mark 11:23

I. Poverty mindset

What is your mindset? What do you see? Do you see yourself poor, struggling or prospering?

a) You will become what you behold. 2 Corinthians 3:17-18 says, *"But we all, with open face beholding as in a glass the glory of the Lord, are changed into the same image from glory to glory, even as by the Spirit of the Lord."*

b) *"Eat thou not the bread of him that hath an evil eye, neither desire thou his dainty meats: For as he **thinketh** in his heart, so is he: Eat and drink, saith he to thee; but his heart is not with thee."* –Proverbs 23:6-7

c) A continued repentance from our poverty mindset is key to experiencing true wealth. Our financial blueprint is a result of what we see, hear, think and experience.

d) A renewed mind concerning wealth is a better asset than money. Our mindset or mind is the difference between lack and increase. There are a lot of "poor" people with plenty of money because of their mindset (wealthy mindset versus a poverty mindset). When someone with a wealthy mindset hits a financial wall, it's only a matter of time before he gets back up because he never lost his millionaire/billionaire mindset. The mindset is key.

See yourself as God sees you. God sees you the way He sees Jesus (John 17:23), as Jesus is right now, so are we also (1 John 4:17).

Chapter Nine

Does God Hate Gay People?

God forbid! This question shows that probably the person asking does not know God, His true nature, or doesn't have a relationship with Him. Why would God hate gay people? This question also clearly shows that the person who is asking it has a preconceived notion about God that is not accurate. Why would God hate the very people He came to die for?

The Bible teaches clearly that God is love (1 John 4:8). The challenge we have today is that there is a perverted type of love that is promoted out there. This kind of love is not God's kind of love that the Bible teaches. Love is not always doing something "good" or something that the other person likes. For instance, sometimes love means to defend or to deal with someone who is coming against a loved one because you love your loved one more. If you truly love your wife, you will fight anyone who comes against her to kill her. If you truly have a good friend, that friend should be willing to tell you the truth even when it hurts or even when you do not want to hear it.

There is a huge difference between the two–the sinner or the sin. We live in times where sin is promoted, applauded, and celebrated. If you hate sin and evil like the Bible teaches (Proverbs 8:13; Psalm 97:10), if you aren't careful, you might end up hating both the sinner and the sin. We have to renew our minds and not slip into hating the sinner and the sin. Do not throw the baby out with the bath water.

Satan is a spirit and needs a physical body to do his evil. This means people will be vessels and instruments through which evil and sin comes. People make themselves available to Satan to work and live through them. Therefore, sometimes we must deal with a person to deal with Satan because that person has yielded himself to the enemy.

We are not against the people, but we must deal with the person in order to deal with sin and evil. This doesn't mean we hate the person, but we hate the sin coming through them. We can't promote or elevate vessels of sin in the effort to love the sinner. Another way of saying this is that we have to deal with sin even if a person gets in the way. Take for instance how government authority does this. They will lock your flesh up if you break the law. They don't hate you, but they hate what you did and the best way for them to stop and restrain you from doing that bad thing they hate is to lock you up. They also love the people you might harm and injure so much that they deal with you to protect them.

If a doctor has to deal with cancer and stop it from spreading and destroying the entire body, he may have to amputate a limb, not because he hates you, but because he loves you so much. He hates cancer, so he will do anything to destroy those cancer cells even if it means damage to your physical body.

A. Jesus hated the sin, not the sinner.

    a) Cast out the scorner.

"Cast out the scorner, and contention shall go out; yea, strife and reproach shall cease."

                                       –Proverbs 22:10

        i) This verse clearly instructs us to deal with the scorner (proud) person so that contention, strife, and reproach might stop. When such a step is done, it's because the person yielded to Satan and is bringing destruction. If we do not deal with him, we will have even bigger problems. We do not deal with him because we hate him, but because we hate the contention, strife, and reproach, and the only way to get rid of it all is by dealing with them.

b) Get thee behind me, Satan.

"Then Peter took him, and began to rebuke him, saying, Be it far from thee, Lord: this shall not be unto thee. But he turned, and said unto Peter, Get thee behind me, Satan: thou art an offence unto me: for thou savourest not the things that be of God, but those that be of men."

–Matthew 16:22-23

    i)   Jesus was not rebuking Peter and calling him Satan. Jesus was looking behind the scene. Satan had inspired Peter to speak this way. The Lord was never against Peter. He loved Peter and prior to this verse He had just given him one of the best compliments. However, at this point in time, Satan was influencing Peter, so Jesus said, "GET thee behind me Satan".

c) Woman at the well

"The woman answered and said, I have no husband. Jesus said unto her, Thou hast well said, I have no husband: For thou hast had five husbands; and he whom thou now hast is not thy husband: in that saidst thou truly."

–John 4:17-18

    i)   These verses are quite interesting. Jesus did not condemn the woman, but He also did not withhold from speaking the truth to her. He loved the sinner (woman) but spoke up against her sin of living in sexual immorality with a man that was not her husband.

    ii) Notice that Jesus said that this man was not her husband. Cohabitating is not a marriage relationship. It doesn't matter how long you have lived together, that man or woman is not your husband or wife.

    iii) I really believe that we can come across very graciously by speaking the truth in love (Ephesians 4:15), but I'm not bound by how people perceive how I come across because they have a choice to perceive it any way they want to.

d) Woman caught in the very act of adultery

"So when they continued asking him, he lifted up himself, and said unto them, He that is without sin among you, let him first cast a stone at her. When Jesus had lifted up himself, and saw none but the woman, he said unto her, Woman, where are those thine accusers? hath no man condemned thee? She said, No man, Lord. And Jesus said unto her, Neither do I condemn thee: go, and sin no more."

–John 8:7, 10-11

   i) This is another good one. This woman is caught in the very act of adultery but when she was brought to Jesus for judgment, His response was quite stunning to these religious men. He said that he that is without sin should cast the first stone at her. Of course, all these religious people had sin, so no one had a right to cast a stone at her among all the people present, but Jesus.

   ii) Jesus valued this woman but not the sin, that's why He said to her, *"go and sin no more."*

We need to hate the act not the actor–the sin not the sinner!

e) Right balance for loving the sinner

In an effort to love the sinner, our society and churches have lost the balance and have ended up damaging people. For instance, promoting homosexuality in churches is detrimental to our children. We should not promote that which, in the end, destroys our children. We shouldn't promote sexual immorality which in turn destroys marriages and homes. I'm not and I will not promote a certain behavior to appear loving to the sinner. I will love the sinner and so should you, but we must hate sin (Psalm 97:10; Proverbs 8:13).

Jesus loves **you** homosexual, **you** thief, **you** liar, and **you** adulterer, but he hates homosexuality, theft, deception, and adultery. He loves the sinner (person) but hates the sin (action or behavior).

B. Rebuke thy brother.

"Thou shalt not hate thy brother in thine heart: thou shalt in any wise rebuke thy neighbor, and not suffer sin upon him."

–Leviticus 19:17

a) If we truly love people, we will tell them the truth regardless of the cost. If they choose to leave the church when we speak the truth, let them leave, praise the Lord, Amen. They probably weren't meant to be there. Again, the balance is the heart or attitude in which we share and/or rebuke them. Blind love that never rebukes is not God's kind of love. Sin is so destructive to people and if you really love them like you say you do, then you will do something to stop them from self-destruction.

b) Also, in the effort to love the sinner, many ministers and preachers have been neutralized from speaking up against sin including, adultery, homosexuality, and so forth. The critics say that is judging or condemning other people. Not true! Jesus spoke up against ungodliness and He was not judging or condemning anyone. The difference is in the attitude.

c) Why then, do people feel condemned? What really condemns people is not us but their own hearts and conscience (John 8:9). When people are living ungodly lifestyles, they will do anything to silence any moral voice that tries to set off their God built-in heart moral alarm (Romans 1:18-22) on the inside of them. This is the very reason people hate churches, Christians, crosses, Christian billboards, prayer in schools, and anything "Jesus tagged", godly and so forth. All of these set off that God built-in heart moral alarm. They are living their lives in rebellion to God, and their hearts condemn them (1John 3:20-21). It's not the cross, not the church, not Jesus Christ, not prayer in schools that condemns people.

True, we can speak against all this ungodliness in a loving way and help people become free–but this doesn't mean all people will come out or get free from such behaviors. Ultimately people choose how they want to behave.

C. Hate sin.

A person that is truly a loving person has to hate sin. If you don't hate adultery, murder, homosexuality, and sin in general you aren't following the Word of God. I have not come across a single scripture that tells you to hate the sinner. Even from the example of Jesus, we see that He loved the sinner and hated the sin.

a) *"Ye that love the LORD, hate evil: he preserveth the souls of his saints; he delivereth them out of the hand of the wicked."* –Psalm 97:10

b) *"The fear of the LORD is to hate evil: pride, and arrogancy, and the evil way, and the froward mouth, do I hate."* –Proverbs 8:13

Jesus loves the sinner so much that He came and died for our sins (Romans 5:8; 2 Corinthians 5:17-21). He loves us and wants to have a relationship with us. The key to stopping the rise of sin is to receive Jesus in our hearts as Lord and Savior. Romans 10:9-10 says, *"That if thou shalt confess with thy mouth the Lord Jesus, and shalt believe in thine heart that God hath raised him from the dead, thou shalt be saved. For with the heart man believeth unto righteousness; and with the mouth confession is made unto salvation. For the scripture saith, whosoever believeth on him shall not be ashamed."*

When we believe on Jesus as our Lord and Savior, we become born again and receive a brand new heart which cannot sin.

Chapter Ten

How Should I Pray for My Loved Ones Who Aren't Saved?

One of the most misunderstood subjects is how to get our loved ones saved. People do not get born again through prayer but through the Word of God. Although prayer is important, it is not a substitute for speaking the Word. If people could be born again through prayer, then why did Jesus tell us to go into all the world and preach the good news making disciples? He would have said just prayed and people would have been saved, but those were not His instructions.

> **"Being born again, not of corruptible seed, but of incorruptible, by the Word of God**, which liveth and abideth forever."
>
> —1 Peter 1:23 (emphasis mine.)

> "So, then faith cometh by hearing, and **hearing by the Word of God.**"
>
> —Romans 10:17 (emphasis mine)

The Word is very clear that faith comes by hearing the Word. So, as we pray, we must keep in mind that we are praying mostly for the Word to get to those we are praying for. It could be first through us or through other ministers, TV, radio waves, one on one, through friends, or through a preacher, or anything or anyone that God can find fit to reach them, etc.

I also must say that we should not carry the burden of our loved one's salvation. We were not created and meant to carry a burden of another person's salvation. This is not to say that we should not have the desire to see them saved, but that we should not have the worry and burden that comes with it. Each person has a choice and free will (Deuteronomy 30:19). Your *will* cannot override their *will*. It is not a wise decision to carry a burden that God told us to cast upon Him (1 Peter 5:6-7). We should pray from a place of peace, not fear or worry, because God wants our loved ones saved more than we do (2 Peter 3:9; 1 Timothy 2:3-4). Matter of fact, He died on the cross for all of them (1 John 2:2) which shows His heart for them even before they were born. He was motivated to die on the cross for our loved ones before we even prayed for them (John 3:16).

The Word is the seed (Mark 4:14; Luke 8:11); the heart of men is the soil (ground). Faith and prayer represent the water that goes along with that seed into the soil.

It is important to understand that the enemy has blinded their eyes so that they cannot believe the gospel and be saved. Satan is working overtime to keep the unsaved lost and blinded lest they come to the knowledge of the Gospel of Christ.

a) *"He hath blinded their eyes, and hardened their heart; that they should not see with their eyes, nor understand with their heart, and be converted, and I should heal them."* –John 12:40.

b) *"But if our gospel be hid, it is hid to them that are lost: In whom the god of this world hath blinded the minds of them which believe not, lest the light of the glorious gospel of Christ, who is the image of God, should shine unto them."* –2 Corinthians 4:3-4

A. Take your authority over the devil.

Many believers do not know of their God-given authority, but even those who know it do not use it to pray for their loved ones. Therefore, because of this ignorance, many miss the opportunity of exercising their authority, thereby running the devil off their loved ones and friends.

a) *"Verily I say unto you, whatsoever ye shall bind on earth shall be bound in heaven: and whatsoever ye shall loose on earth shall be loosed in heaven."* –Matthew 18:18

i) This verse also gives tremendous authority to bind and loose. We can bind the devil and we can loose the captives free from his oppression. What we bind and loose on earth, heaven is in agreement.

b) *"Then he called his twelve disciples together, and gave them power and authority over all devils, and to cure diseases."* –Luke 9:1

i) We have been given power and authority over all devils. Not over a few, not over some, but all.

B. Open the eyes of their understanding.

"That the God of our Lord Jesus Christ, the Father of glory, may give unto you the spirit of wisdom and revelation in the knowledge of him: The eyes of your understanding being enlightened; that ye may know what is the hope of his calling, and what the riches of the glory of his inheritance in the saints."

–Ephesians 1:17-18

For someone to come to the knowledge of Christ, their eyes of understanding have to be opened. This scripture is an example of how we should pray. We should pray that God will open or enlighten their eyes so that they can understand and believe the Gospel. This is a valid way to pray for our loved ones.

C. Laborers in the fields

"Then saith he unto his disciples, the harvest truly is plenteous, but the labourers are few; Pray ye therefore the Lord of the harvest, that he will send forth labourers into his harvest."

–Matthew 9:37-38

The key to people getting saved is hearing the Gospel, because faith comes by hearing (Romans 10:17), but how shall they hear if they have not been sent (Romans 10:14). This is one of the most powerful scriptures to always remember and pray for our loved ones and friends. We should pray that God will send workers such as ministers, preachers, missionaries, and friends to our loved ones, that they will listen to them when they will not listen to us.

D. Holy scriptures known from childhood

"And that from a child thou hast known the holy scriptures, which are able to make thee wise unto salvation through faith which is in Christ Jesus."

–2 Timothy 3:15

Most people were either raised in church or were taught some scriptures at an early stage of their lives. Therefore, this scripture can be a foundation for praying that God would bring those scriptures to remembrance or to light to our loved ones. We can also pray that the Lord would remind them of how good He has been to them over the years and how He has looked out for them.

E. Boldness to speak the Word

Sometimes all we need is the boldness to speak the Word and speak to our loved ones and friends. We tend to be fearful and we end up playing it safe in fear of rejection or ridicule. Sometimes we are so fearful of what might not happen. Some people will receive from us and through us, but some will not.

"And now, Lord, behold their threatenings: and grant unto thy servants, that with all boldness they may speak thy word."

–Acts 4:29

Notice that Peter prayed for boldness to speak the Word. We can also pray for boldness to speak the Word of God to our loved ones. We do not have to fear.

F. Come to the end of themselves

"And when he came to himself, he said, How many hired servants of my father's have bread enough and to spare, and I perish with hunger! I will arise and go to my father, and will say unto him, Father, I have sinned against heaven, and before thee."

–Luke15:17-18

Many times, all it takes for some people to arise and head towards the Lord is that they come to the end of themselves, or that they come to realize they can do it no more by their own strength. Sometimes the best way to look up is by lying flat on your back. The prodigal son came to the end of himself, then came to his senses.

G. Revelation of the love of God

The Word of God teaches that it is the goodness of God that leads men to repentance (Romans 2:4). We can pray that our lost loved ones will come to the knowledge and understanding of the love of God and the goodness of God, which will in turn lead them to repentance.

Although it is true some people can get born again through the fear of hell, this is not the primary way God wins people over to His kingdom. He does it by love. We can draw more bees by honey than vinegar. The good news (gospel) is the power of God unto salvation to those that believe, be it Jew or Gentile (Romans 1:17).

"And to know the love of Christ, which passeth knowledge, that ye might be filled with all the fullness of God."

–Ephesians 3:18

"No man can come to me, except the Father which hath sent me draw him: and I will raise him up at the last day."

–John 6:44

Prayer:

Abba Father, Thank You for the Lord Jesus and the finished work at the cross. Your Word clearly shows that Your heart is for ALL men to be saved and come to repentance. Thank You for dying for our sins and those of our friends and loved ones. I pray that the Holy Spirit will draw them in by Your love. I pray that their hearts will be softened to receive and believe the Word. I pray that You will send forth laborers and other Christians across their path that will speak the Word and share the love of Jesus with them. Father use anything and anyone who is in relationship with them to point them towards You and Your love for them. Open their eyes as You speak to them through songs, radio, TV, books, the Bible, creation, and so forth. Bring to memory and remembrance the acts of love You have done for them in the past and the scriptures that they have heard or been taught in the past. I bind the influence and the work of the enemy that has been blinding them to the good news and the love of God, in Jesus' name. I speak to those blinders to come down and to come off their eyes and hearts, in Jesus' name. I declare that their hearts are soft and willing to receive the Word of God that brings about salvation, and I also pray that faith is born as they hear the Word, in Jesus' name. Thank you, Lord that you want them saved more than I do. Hallelujah. Thank You, Jesus.

Chapter Eleven

Is Jesus the Only Way?

If you wanted to come to my house and you did not know how to get there and the address to my house, would you take any way you want to get there? Of course not! All roads would not lead you to my house and you would not want to come up with various strange ways to get there. In the same way if we want to make it to heaven, we do not come up with just any directions to get there. If you wanted to make it to my house, you would have to ask me for directions because I know my house address and you do not. It would be insanity for you to think you can just come up with directions to my house. It wouldn't work. There is a specific direction that would get you to my house and you would have to follow it to get there.

In the same way, God is giving us directions to His house and how we can get there. That is ONLY through Jesus. Jesus is the only way to God and relationship with Him. Any other way is going to lead people to the wrong place. We can't just come up with any directions hoping that they will lead us there. It doesn't work that way.

John 14:6 says, ***"Jesus saith unto him, I am the way, the truth, and the life: no man cometh unto the Father, but by me."***

A. The only way

This verse says that there are not many paths to God. Jesus is the only way and there is no other way. God's only way of salvation is through Jesus (Acts 4:12). Any other religion such as evolution, Buddhism, Islam, Hinduism, witchcraft, and many more will only eternally damn people. They are manmade religions. However, Christianity is not a religion but a relationship with God through Jesus Christ the Savior. We are the only one that boasts a Savior. We are the only one that has our sins forgiven by putting faith in Jesus our Savior. No other religion can boast that. We are the only one with an assurance of salvation and eternal life. All religions are not even sure of salvation, it's like "we will see when we get there." We are also the only one that does not make people carry or pay for their own sins by placing them on their backs, because no one can. We are the only one that receives salvation and forgiveness by only BELIEVING, not by performance and doing.

The Word of God doesn't say, "whosoever obeys Him perfectly", it doesn't say "whoever never fails again", and it certainly doesn't say "whoever keeps all His commandments". It simply says, "whoever believes in Him." Whoever believes in Him will not perish but have eternal life. The only action needed on your part is to believe and receive.

Faith in Jesus is so different from all other religions. Many of these religions get offended, but the truth is that faith in Jesus is different from all other religions because it is the only way.

   a) Jesus's claims leave no other option for salvation. Remember, He did not say He was "A way, A truth, and A life," but He claimed to be the ONLY way, the ONLY truth, and the ONLY life.

B. Some people feel it's not fair for God to say there is only one way to Him. Man wants to find his own way to God, but this has not worked very well. If Jesus said He was the only way, the truth, and the life, why should people dispute that? He lived a life of truth and proved it furthermore when he predicted his death and resurrection (John 2:19; Luke 9:22; Matthew 16:21).

a) If Jesus was a liar, He would have told the people around him that He would resurrect spiritually not bodily because there would be no proof for His spiritual resurrection. However, He told the folks that He would resurrect bodily (physical) and it happened and was seen by many people (1 Corinthians 15:6). A physical resurrection has a visible proof unlike a spiritual resurrection. Jesus rose physically in a body, visibly, and tangibly.

C. All the enemies of Jesus could not find any sin in His life, so they made up false accusations. Luke 23:4 says that *"Then said Pilate to the chief priests and to the people, I find no fault in this man."* Even Pilate as ungodly as he was could not find any fault in Jesus. What a testimony! John 8:46 **"Which of you con vinceth me of sin? And if I say the truth, why do ye not believe me?"**

D. **Through creation, God has surrounded us with "one-ways". Our lives are full of "one-ways". They are all around us.**

For example:

a) Why would Jesus come to die if there were multiple ways? He came because there was no other way and He opened the only way. If there was another way, Jesus wouldn't have come. There was no, and there is no other way.

b) Driving only on one side of the road.

c) The sun rises east and sets west. This happens in only one way 365 days and never changes.

d) One sun, moon etc.

e) Your gas tank takes only gasoline or diesel but not both.

f) One father, one mother.

Creation is screaming that there is only one way. Why is it troubling for people to believe that there is only one way to God? Jesus is the one and only way!

If I wanted you to come to my house and I knew you didn't know how to get there, I'd have to tell you how to get to my house. You don't come up with a way to get to a place you do not know or have never been. You need one who has been there to direct you there. If you just take any road saying there are many ways to my house, you will never get there. You may enjoy the ride, but you will end up in a wrong place. Jesus is the only way!

E. **Jesus pointed to His signs and wonders as another reason people should believe in Him.**

There were some—magicians and false prophets—who did "miracles" in the day of Jesus and others who will in the future (Matthew 24:24), but there was something different about Jesus' miracles. They were intended for Him to point people to a miracle as a sign for them to believe that He was who He claimed to be. Jesus was confident in trusting the authenticity of His miracles to the point that He encouraged people to believe in Him because of them.

a) John 10:38 *"But if I do, though ye believe not me, believe the works: that ye may know, and believe, that the Father is in me, and I in him."*

b) John 14:11 *"Believe me that I am in the Father, and the Father in me: or else believe me for the very works' sake."*

If you are looking for a reason to believe in Jesus (and you should), I have given you plenty. **Jesus is THE WAY, THE TRUTH, and THE LIFE.**

Chapter Twelve

I'm a Good Person, Will I Go to Heaven?

Most people believe that all it takes to make it into heaven is their good works and performance, but the hard truth is that no man can deserve God's blessing through his actions. Even under the OT, no one was blessed because they obeyed God perfectly. The blood of a sacrificial lamb was instituted as a temporary measure to remit the sins of the people, but it was not their good deeds and perfect performance that caused them to be blessed. All of us owed or owe a debt we can never pay.

> "And Jesus said unto him, why callest thou me good? **there is none good but one, that is, God.**"
>
> –Mark 10:18 (emphasis mine)

This verse clearly teaches that only God is good. Good people do not go to heaven, it's people who are born again (saved) or in other words have accepted and received Jesus as their Lord and Savior that go to heaven. Some of these might be really good people, but the reason they make it to heaven is not based on how good they are, but on faith–believing in Jesus as Savior.

This might be a shock to you if you think you are a good person, but it's true. If being good is the reason to go to heaven, then how good are you supposed to be? What is the standard for that goodness? And how do you know you have met that standard? The Bible teaches us how to clearly make it into heaven. If you owned heaven, you would be the only one to set the standard and the way people can come in. God made it clear enough that Jesus is the only way to make it into heaven (John 14:6).

Romans 3:23 says, *"For all have sinned, and come short of the glory of God."* All men have sinned and sin, therefore none of them are good. Goodness is not the basis for relationship with God but faith in Jesus. So, if heaven is your only goal, then you MUST make Jesus the Lord and Savior of your life. There is no other way. You can't come up with your own way to enter heaven, but you must follow the instructions and directions of the owner.

Additionally, there is more to life than just going to heaven. The Lord wants you to experience an abundant life here in this life, not just in heaven. He wants you well, peaceful, healthy, wealthy, prosperous, delivered, and fulfilling your purpose. He wants to have a personal relationship with you even in this life, and not only in the one to come (Heaven).

> *"And when he was gone forth into the way, there came one running, and kneeled to him, and asked him, Good Master, what shall I do that I may inherit eternal life? And Jesus said unto him, Why callest thou me good? There is none good but one, that is, God. Thou knoweth the commandments, Do not commit adultery, Do not kill, Do not steal, Do not bear false witness, Defraud not, Honor thy father and mother. And he answered and said unto him, Master, all these have I observed from my youth. Then Jesus beholding him loved him, and said unto him, One thing thou lackest: go thy way, sell whatsoever thou hast, and give to the poor, and thou shalt have treasure in heaven: and come, take up the cross, and follow me. And he was sad at that saying, and went away grieved: for he had great possessions."*
>
> –Mark 10:17-22

This young man who came to Jesus was saying he was good and that he had kept all the law. He trusted in his goodness thinking that he would enter into relationship with God based on his goodness. To his surprise, he found out that he couldn't after Jesus made this clear. If you keep the whole law and yet break one, you have broken every piece of it (James 2:10). You are guilty of breaking all of it. So, then who can keep the law? No man can. Only Jesus (God Incarnate) kept the law completely and fulfilled it. The only way any other man keeps the law is by believing in Jesus as their Lord and Savior, who actually kept the law.

There is one major thing that separates Christians from all other religions. Unlike other religions, Christianity teaches that you do not have to be good or a good person to enter into relationship with God. 1 Timothy 4:10 *"For therefore we both labor and suffer reproach,* **because we trust in the living God, who is the Savior of all men, especially of those that believe"** (emphasis mine).

It's not our good acts and deeds that will save us and purchase us a ticket into heaven, but only faith in Jesus Christ. We are saved by grace through faith (Ephesians 2:8-9). NO one is saved by their good deeds. Even the good deeds of man still come short of God's standard of goodness. The Word of God doesn't say "whosoever obeys Him perfectly", it doesn't say "whoever never fails again". And it certainly doesn't say "whoever keeps all His commandments." It simply says, whoever **believes** in Him will not perish but have eternal life. The only action needed on your part is to believe and receive.

"Therefore, by the deeds of the law there shall no flesh be justified in his sight." (Romans 3:20). Also, Romans 3:28 says, *"Therefore we conclude that a man is justified by faith without the deeds of the law."*

"Deeds of the law" refer to our good deeds and trusting in them as a means of relationship with God. We are justified by faith, not by our good works. Man, at his best, is still not good. If you think you are a good person, your goodness is as filthy rags before God. Isaiah 64:6 *"But we are all as an unclean thing, and all our righteousnesses are as filthy rags; and we all do fade as a leaf; and our iniquities, like the wind, have taken us away."* All men need Jesus. Relationship with Jesus is the key to heaven. Jesus paid for all the sins of the world. (1 John 2:2: *"And he is the propitiation for our sins: and not for ours only, but also for the sins of the whole world."*) All you have to do is believe and receive.

Romans 10:9-10 *says,* *"That if thou shalt confess with thy mouth the Lord Jesus, and shalt* **believe in thine heart that God hath raised him from the dead**, *thou* *shalt be saved. For with the heart man **believeth unto righteousness**; and with the mouth confession is made unto salvation. For the scripture saith, whosoever believeth on him shall not be ashamed. For there is no difference between the Jew and the Greek: for the same Lord over all is rich unto all that call upon him. For whosoever shall call upon the name of the Lord shall be saved."* (emphasis mine)

a) These verses say that we must believe with the heart. Head knowledge and acknowledgement is not believing. After we have believed with the heart, then we are to confess. Confession alone will not save a person. This has to be a heart commitment and belief.

b) We need to profess or confess what we possess.

c) If we have truly believed, we shall confess–sooner or later. It is impossible for one to believe on the Lord Jesus and never say so. Truly faith will be seen in confession and action–behavior.

d) We do not become righteous by performance but by believing. We can't work our way into righteousness with God.

e) Romans 10:9-10. Two main things we need to believe to be saved.

   i) Who He is and was

     • Lord Jesus–Lord (Divinity).

     • Jesus (Humanity).

Note: **Every cult gets the person of Jesus wrong.**

   ii) What He did

     • Died and rose from the dead.

     • **Believe in thine heart that God hath raised him from the dead.** No one can be born again unless they believe that Jesus rose again from the dead. This is a crucial aspect of the gospel.

If you believe in your heart that God raised Him from the dead, confessing this with your mouth, you will be saved–born again. For whosoever person shall call upon the name of the Lord shall be saved. Are you a "whosoever"? You qualify. Believe on Jesus and His finished work at the cross.

Chapter Thirteen

Does God Speak? If Yes, How Does He Speak?

One of the most important aspects of a believer's walk with God is the ability to hear His voice. This will save us many heartaches and many pitfalls. God wants to speak to us, and He is continually speaking to us to give us direction, but many of us are not listening.

God is always speaking. He is not talkative, but He is always communicating with us. It is not a matter that He is not speaking. It's a matter of us not tuning in, listening and understanding.

There are two main types of guidance:

a) General guidance

    i) God gives us His general will for us in every area–spiritually and naturally.

    ii) Psalm 119:105–The Word.

    iii) Disobeying the general guidance/God's will in the Word will hinder us from receiving the specific will or guidance.

    iv) Examples of God's general guidance are:

        • Thanksgiving: *"In every thing give thanks: for this is the will of God in Christ Jesus concerning you."* –1 Thessalonians 5:18

- Sanctification–abstaining from fornication

  "For this is the will of God, even your sanctification, that ye should abstain from fornication:" –1 Thessalonians 4:3

- Renewing our mind

  "I beseech you therefore, brethren, by the mercies of God, that ye present your bodies a living sacrifice, holy, acceptable unto God, which is your reasonable service. And be not conformed to this world: but be ye transformed by the renewing of your mind, that ye may prove what is that good, and acceptable, and perfect, will of God." –Romans 12:1-2

- Not willing that any perish

  "The Lord is not slack concerning his promise, as some men count slackness; but is longsuffering to us-ward, not willing that any should perish, but that all should come to repentance." –2 Peter 3:9

b) Specific guidance

   i) This is through the Holy Spirit.

   - Example: Thess. 3:10 tells us to **work**, but it doesn't say where or what, but it is the Holy Spirit who tells us where to work and what. This is specific guidance.

   - Another example is marriage. The Word of God (general guidance) encourages us to marry and teaches us to marry only the opposite sex. However, it doesn't tell us to marry anyone or who to marry specifically apart from the general guidance that we should marry a believer in the Lord (2 Corinthians 6:14). It is the Holy Spirit that gives us those specifics–who to marry and when.

"My sheep hear my voice, and I know them, and they follow me:"
                                                    –John 10:27

Here are some of the ways in which God speaks to us:

A. God's Word

God's Word is the number one way God speaks and leads us. We should desire to have God speak to us through His written Word. As we study and read, we should be expecting God to speak to us.

a) *"And they said one to another, Did not our heart burn within us, while he talked with us by the way, and **while he opened to us the scriptures**?"* –Luke 24:32

    i) He (God) **talks** to us while He opens **the scriptures (The Word)**. We need to be in the Word if we want Him to talk to us.

b) *"Through thy precepts I get understanding: therefore I hate every false way. Thy word is a lamp unto my feet, and a light unto my path."* –Psalms 119:104-105

c) The primary way God speaks to us is through His Word. Whenever we think we have heard from God, we must give that "word" an **acid test of the Word**. If it fails to pass the Word test, then it is not God, period. I don't care how it sounds or feels.

d) God will NEVER EVER violate His Word. Psalm 138:2 says *"I will worship toward thy holy temple, and praise thy name for thy lovingkindness and for thy truth: for thou hast magnified thy word above all thy name."*

e) Notice that John 10:27 says that **we do know and do hear God's voice**. It doesn't say we can know, or we should know, but **we know**. It doesn't say we can hear, or we will hear, but that we do hear His voice.

f) As you read the Word, you will receive a "Rhema" Word. ("Rhema" is a Greek word which means utterance" or "thing said". This is a Word that is quickened to you, jumps off the page as you read and speaks directly to you and/or your situation.

g) *"The integrity of the upright shall guide them: but the perverseness of transgressors shall destroy them."* –Proverbs 11:3

  i) Integrity will guide us. If we walk in integrity, we have guidance from the Lord, because God's voice and direction will be one of integrity.

We need to filter all guidance and voices through the Word of God.

B. Revelation knowledge

This way by which God speaks to us is tied to God's Word.

As we study the Word, God will speak to us by giving us a revelation of something we did not know about or could not have known by ourselves in the natural. This could be instructions or guidance of any sort.

C. Spirit

It is important to understand that we are a spirit being. When God speaks to us, He speaks to our spirit man who then communicates to our soul and mind.

a) *"God is a Spirit: and they that worship him must worship him in spirit and in truth."* –John 4:24

b) God speaks to our spirit. He is a Spirit, and when He communicates to us, He does it Spirit to spirit. And since we are one Spirit with the Lord (1 Corinthians 6:17), our born-again spirit is the very Spirit of God. So, God communicates to the Spirit of God in us. He doesn't communicate to us mouth to ear or brain to brain, like in the physical or emotional realms.

D. Faith

One of the hindrances to hearing God's voice is unbelief. Some do not believe that they hear or have heard God's voice. Just like our daily walk with God in all aspects of life, **it takes faith to hear God's voice**. We live by faith (Habakkuk 2:4).

Everything in the kingdom of God operates on faith. Healing, speaking in tongues, salvation, deliverance, provision, hearing God's voice–everything!

We have to step out in faith and believe that we are being led and have heard God's voice, and, on many occasions, we will get confirmation that this is true. Of course, this voice should not and cannot violate the written Word of God.

    a) Romans 14:23 tells us *"...for whatsoever is not of faith is sin."*

        i) We have to be decisive when we hear God. We have to step out and act on what we believe God has spoken to us by faith.

    b) Inaction is no excuse. Hebrews 11:6 says that without faith it is IMPOSSIBLE to please God. So, we have to step out and act in faith. Everything we will ever do in the kingdom of God requires walking by faith.

E. Heart Desires

One of the ways we hear God's voice, or we can be led by God, is through our heart desires. Most believers have no clue that on some occasions it is the Lord leading them through their heart desires, but this is true, and it happens more often than not.

    a) *"Delight thyself also in the Lord: and he shall give thee the desires of thine heart."* –Psalm 37:4

    b) This does not really apply to a person who has not been seeking the Lord. To trust and follow the desires of your heart, you must be in continual fellowship with God, not your flesh. If you aren't careful, then your flesh and/or the devil could speak to you through your desires.

    c) You must be delighting yourself in the Lord. To *"delight"* comes from the Hebrew Word "ANAG" which means "to be soft and pliable" (Strong's Concordance). So, this scripture is saying that we must soften and make our hearts sensitive towards the Lord. This doesn't just happen automatically. It takes lots of effort. If our hearts aren't soft and sensitive towards the Lord, we should never DO whatever we want.

d) This is not saying that God will give us whatever we want. It is saying that when we delight (be soft and pliable) ourselves in the Lord, He will change our heart desires to be identical to His and will meet those desires. In other words, he will place His desires into our hearts, and we will have God desires.

e) Ungodly desires in our heart are an indication of hardness and insensitivity of our hearts towards the Lord.

   i) If you have a desire and you aren't sure it's the Lord, back off, pray and fast. If that desire stays and gets stronger, this could be a clear indication that the Lord is speaking to you.

f) Mr. Andrew Wommack says he made some of the most important decisions of his life by using this pattern. He followed the desires of his heart to go on TV and the same to start one of the best Bible Colleges in the world–Charis Bible College.

As we seek God (delight in Him), He puts godly desires in our hearts. Those desires are His plan, will, and direction. They are constant and persistent.

Maybe you are asking yourself, why am I not hearing anything significant? "If you are praying and seeking Me and you don't hear anything specific it is because you already have My mind on the matter. I trust you. Do what you feel is best in your heart."

–Pastor Greg Mohr

F. "Seemer"

Another one of the ways we hear God's voice, or we can be led by God is through our "seemer". This is something that seems good to us. Most believers have no clue that on some occasions it is the Lord leading them when something seems good to them, but this is true, and it happens more often than not.

a) *"Forasmuch as many have taken in hand to set forth in order a declaration of those things which are most surely believed among us, Even as they delivered them unto us, which from the beginning were eyewitnesses, and ministers of the word;* **It seemed good to me** *also, having had perfect understanding of all things from the very first, to write unto thee in order, most excellent Theophilus, That thou mightest know the certainty of those things, wherein thou hast been instructed."* –Luke 1:1-4

b) Being led by your "seemer" is best for a person who is seeking after the Lord continually. This will not work well for carnal people. Proverbs 14:12 says, *"There is a way that seemeth right to a man, but the ends thereof are the ways of Death."*

c) *"It seemed good unto us, being assembled with one accord, to send chosen men unto you with our beloved Barnabas and Paul."* –Acts 15:25

d) *"For it seemed good to the Holy Ghost, and to us, to lay upon you no greater burden than these necessary things."* –Acts 15:28

G. "Pleaser"

This is more like the previous one ("seemer"). Another one of the ways we hear God's voice, or we can be led by God is through our "pleaser". This is something that pleases us.

a) *"Notwithstanding it **pleased** Silas to abide there still."* –Acts 15:34

b) *"Then **pleased** it the apostles and elders, with the whole church, to send chosen men of their own company to Antioch with Paul and Barnabas: namely, Judas surnamed Barsabas, and Silas, chief men among the brethren."* –Acts 15:22

H. Inner Witness

When God speaks to us, one of the ways is through an inner witness of the Holy Spirit. The inner witness is the number one way God leads His children into His specific will.

What is a witness? It is simply a thing or voice furnishing evidence or proof. The inner witness will eliminate all other voices. This could be a voice that is repetitive and comes with a strong conviction. It can also be a strong conviction about something.

> *"The Spirit itself beareth witness with our spirit, that we are the children of God: And if children, then heirs; heirs of God, and joint-heirs with Christ; if so be that we suffer with him, that we may be also glorified together."*
>
> –Romans 8:16-17

a) The Holy Spirit will bear witness to His will, the things that He wants us to see and know through our spirit man. Some things will bear witness while others will not.

b) This witness could be for or against something, a red light or a green light. It could be a **check** in your spirit, an impression or a thought. Have you ever had a thought that comes randomly? That spontaneous thought is not always spectacular but can be supernatural.

c) When God speaks to you, it will bear witness with your spirit man. There will be a Spirit to spirit connection. He is not bearing witness with our eyes, minds, etc., but our spirit.

d) *"The spirit of man is the candle of the LORD, searching all the inward parts of the belly."* –Proverbs 20:27

I. Peace

This is one of the primary keys to being led by God, hearing, and following His direction. Nothing should be worth taking our peace. We need our peace to function soberly and make sound judgment. Something that takes your peace away has to be put on the shelf, dropped or ignored. If peace is gone, it is time to back off.

Sometimes we take the uncomfortableness of the flesh to be the voice of God. Sometimes we are being stretched and there tends to be a lack of "peace." On many occasions, it is the flesh that is screaming for not wanting to change or suffer any loss, not the voice of God.

a) *"And let the peace of God rule in your hearts, to the which also ye are called in one body; and be ye thankful."* –Colossians 3:15

  i) The word "rule" here means "to act as an umpire" (Strong's concordance). An umpire helps decide or determine the direction of a point. Whether the point is in bounds or outbounds, positive or negative, green light to a point or red light to a point.

  ii) Peace is God's umpire for making decisions.

b) God speaks to us through the peace in our hearts.

c) We need to consider all the options. Many wrong decisions have been made because not all the options were considered.

d) Don't let fear rule out God's possibilities.

e) Use your imagination to explore what will happen with each choice.

f) Where do you have **the most peace**? God will always lead you in the direction where you have the most peace. Follow the peace of God. Discern **the greater peace** as you consider the option the Lord would have you take. In your spirit, there will be **total peace** over the right choice, but we aren't always totally in the Spirit, and it is not unusual for some turmoil to exist.

g) Peace is the timing of what God wants to do. Don't violate the peace. Passion is the "what."

  i) **During a purchase of a car or house, loans, spouse you marry, etc. for every single decision you will make, God will be there speaking to you.**

h) *"So shall my word be that goeth forth out of my mouth: it shall not return unto me void, but it shall accomplish that which I please, and it shall prosper* *in the thing whereto I sent it. For ye shall go out with joy, **and be led forth with peace:** the mountains and the hills shall break forth before you into singing, and all the trees of the field shall clap their hands."* – Isaiah 55:11-12

J. Passion

*"In addition to peace, Isaiah 55:11-12 also speaks to passion, "So shall my word be that goeth forth out of my mouth: it shall not return unto me void, but it shall accomplish that which I please, and it shall prosper in the thing whereto I sent it. **For ye shall go out with joy**, and be led forth with peace: the mountains and the hills shall break forth before you into singing, and all the trees of the field shall clap their hands."*

– Isaiah 55:11-12

a) The joy in this verse indicates a passion.

b) One of the other primary ways to hear the voice of God is through our **passion or joy**. What are you passionate about? What are you excited about?

c) Remember to not make decisions only based on passion and leave peace behind. You need to remember to operate in the two **"P's"– passion and peace. Passion is the what. Peace is the timing of the "what"**.

d) Most people have passion, but not peace. They tend to follow the passion, leaving peace behind, and hence miss the timing of God.

K. Heart Reservations

The definition of reservation is skepticism, unease, hesitation, hesitancy, reluctance. Heart reservations could be things that you get to know that just bring about certain reservations in your heart. They are more like red flags. This is a crucial way God warns us and can lead us to go a different direction by revealing some information to us that would bring reservations. These should never be ignored.

a) God speaks to us through certain reservations we get about making certain decisions or taking certain steps. Although not all the reservations we have are God speaking to us, we must take time and think through things. Proverbs 4:26 says, *"Ponder the path of thy feet, and let all thy ways be established."*

b) Never neglect nor go against the reservations in your heart (Genesis 27:1-30). Never do it. It is not worth the pain and heartache that will eventually follow.

c) Never force yourself (1 Samuel 13:12) to do something that you have a reservation or red flag on.

L. Kingdom Protocol

The kingdom of God has protocol. There are certain things we have to be looking for to confirm the voice of God and His direction to us.

a) *"For the kingdom of God is not meat and drink; but righteousness, and peace, and joy in the Holy Ghost."* –Romans 14:17

　　i) Righteousness

　　ii) Peace

　　iii) Joy

b) *"But the wisdom that is from above is first pure, then peaceable, gentle, and easy to be intreated, full of mercy and good fruits, without partiality, and without hypocrisy."* –James 3:17

　　i) God's voice will lead us in a direction, and wisdom that fulfills and that is pure, peaceable, gentle, easy to be intreated (willing to yield), full of mercy, good fruits, without partiality and without hypocrisy.

M. Still Small Voice

God's voice is not usually a big audible voice, especially under the New Covenant. Some have heard that audible voice but that is occasional and not the norm. In the Old Covenant, God spoke and communicated with the people externally. One of the reasons for that is that the people weren't born again and they weren't the temple of God, however in the New Covenant, God speaks to us internally because we are the temple of the Holy Spirit and God Himself lives on the inside of us. This was not the case in the Old Covenant as God dwelt outside, not on the inside. God typically speaks to us in a still small voice on the inside of us.

a) *"Be still, and know that I am God: I will be exalted among the heathen, I will be exalted in the earth."* –Psalm 46:10

   i) The word *"still"* comes from a Hebrew word that was translated *"slacken"* This is talking about slowing down, calming down, being quiet, "stepping out of traffic" (MSG).

   ii) Often, we have to be still to hear the voice of God. There are voices in our daily life that compete with the voice of God. We need to create an environment to allow ourselves to hear God's voice.

   iii) One of the reasons we can't hear God's still voice is because we are so busy with life. We have no time for God.

      • We are busy Lord, can't you see? We must deliberately get quiet. I mean quiet.

      • Turn off that television, radio, and any sort of noise and be still. You will hear God's voice. God doesn't yell!

b) *"And after the earthquake a fire; but the Lord was not in the fire: and after the fire a still small voice."* –1 Kings 19:12

   i) God is not always in the spectacular nor dramatic. Here in this situation, God was not in the earthquake nor in the fire but was in the very unexpected–a still small voice.

c) This is not talking about a loud audible voice, but rather a voice deep inside our spirit.

N. Visions, Dreams, Audible Voice.

We should not **seek** visions, dreams, an audible voice, and so forth. All these are secondary forms of God leading us. We ought to solely depend on the Word of God and the inner witness as God's primary way to be led by Him. If the Word of God is not sufficient, nothing else will be.

We may be invited into certain dimensions of the Spirit realm, but **we should never seek it**.

Examples:

a) Paul, (2 Corinthians 12:4) was caught up into the heavens. He did not go into the heavens. He was caught there. He did not go there on his own. He was invited there.

b) **John** in the book of Revelation saw an open door which was a sign of invitation. He never sought it. He was invited into it. Revelation 4:1 *"come up hither and I will shew thee things which must be hereafter."*

c) **We should stop looking for the spectacular or dramatic.**

O. Prophecy

Another way God speaks to us or how we can hear His voice is through prophecy.

Prophecy is simply an inspired word from God in a known tongue that is meant to edify, exhort, and comfort.

The Word of God is clear about NOT despising prophecy (**1 Thessalonians 5:20** *"Despise not prophesyings"*). One of the ways God speaks to us or how we can hear God's voice is through the operation of Spiritual Gifts.

a) *"Now concerning spiritual gifts, brethren, I would not have you ignorant."* —1 Corinthians 12:1

b) *"But he that prophesieth speaketh unto men to edification, and exhortation, and comfort."* —1 Corinthians 14:3

    i) There are three major checks to prophesy or a word of prophecy:

- Edification

- Exhortation

- Comfort

Prophecy is simply an inspired word from God in a known tongue that is meant to edify, exhort, and comfort.

P. Spiritual Authorities

"And he gave some, apostles; and some, prophets; and some, evangelists; and some, pastors and teachers; For the perfecting of the saints, for the work of the ministry, for the edifying of the body of Christ: Till we all come in the unity of the faith, and of the knowledge of the Son of God, unto a perfect man, unto the measure of the stature of the fullness of Christ: That we henceforth be no more children, tossed to and fro, and carried about with every wind of doctrine, by the sleight of men, and cunning craftiness, whereby they lie in wait to deceive."

—Ephesians 4:11-14

a) Sometimes God will use spiritual authorities such as pastors, teachers, elders, evangelists, and so forth to speak into our lives. God does and will give us direction through them. However, there is a balance that has to be met with this. No leader is infallible. No leader is to be obeyed in this regard without any questions.

    i) They are not the final authority, but they can be a witness and a blessing.

ii) We need to keep this in mind concerning counsel. No leader is infallible.

Q. Godly Counsel

This is advice or prudence that could come from another person or from God's Word. This is another way God can lead or speak to us. We should be cautious who we choose to receive counsel from, and definitely avoid the ungodly (Psalm 1:1-3).

We should seek counsel in certain areas which will help us hear God's voice and direction. God speaks through counsel and the Word encourages counsel.

a) We have to be cautious not to get counsel from the ungodly (Psalm 1:1-3).

b) *"Where no counsel is, the people fall: but in the multitude of counsellors there is safety."* –Proverbs 11:14

c) *"Without counsel purposes are disappointed: but in the multitude of counsellors they are established."* –Proverbs 15:22

d) *"Hear counsel, and receive instruction, that thou mayest be wise in thy latter end."* –Proverbs 19:20

e) *"Counsel in the heart of man is like deep water; but a man of understanding will draw it out."* –Proverbs 20:5

f) *"Every purpose is established by counsel: and with good advice make war."* –Proverbs 20:18

g) *"Thou shalt guide me with thy counsel, and afterward receive me to glory."* –Psalm 73:24

Below are crucial points to note about God speaking to us and hearing His voice.

R. Clarity

a) **When God speaks, He speaks clearly.** You will know that you know that you know. If it's blurry, make sure that you get clarity. Pray in the Spirit, study the Word, seek God's direction. **God is the best communicator ever.** He will communicate to us clearly.

b) I believe God speaks and knows every language and dialect on earth. When He speaks to you, **He will speak the language you understand.** He will not sound like someone else, but I believe the voice of **God sounds like you—your voice.**

S. Emotion and Flesh or the Voice of God

Sometimes when we are being stretched, we take that discomfort toward **change to mean we have no peace.**

Change—whether forced or not—can bring negative emotional effects. Internal and external resistance to change will come. Sometimes Christians mistake their feelings of resistance as the voice of God telling them not to change. Feelings of resistance can actually be a sign that you are on the right track.

How do you discern if it is the voice of God or it is the flesh and emotion?

a) The Word

   Example:

   i) When it comes to things like relationships, we have to remember that God's kind of love is patient and doesn't behave itself unseemly.

      • Marrying the unbeliever is against the Word of God (2 Corinthians 6:14) regardless of how we feel. We should not make our decisions based on our emotions. Emotions are real but aren't always true. We should never be led by our emotions. They are unstable and unpredictable.

b) Fasting and prayer

    i) Spending time with the Lord through studying the Word, fasting, and prayer will cause the flesh to be subdued and we will hear the voice of God more clearly.

c) Godly counsel from trusted mature men and women of God

    i) Counsel should help confirm or unconfirm what God is speaking to you, not to tell you what to do.

    ii) A godly counsel will give you guidance, but you will have to make the decision yourself.

T. Confirmation

a) Does it align with God's Word? Is it Christ-exalting or self-promoting? Does it manifest the flesh or the Spirit of God? Are my heart motives pure? Does my mentor or someone I believe is spiritually mature agree to it? Does it require faith?

b) I have noticed that when God speaks to us, we must step out by faith and follow God's Word. We should not be putting out fleeces like Gideon before the Lord (Judges 6:36-40), audible voices, tingling sensations, and so forth.

c) God confirms His Word (Mark 16:20). I believe when He speaks to us, He will confirm it.

    i) We should be careful not to be seeking confirmation. We should seek the Lord and His Word and confirmation will come. God will give us confirmation, but it is unwise to be seeking it. If we do, we are seeking the wrong thing and we could be easily misled.

Let me list some of the difficulties or hindrances of hearing God:

    i) Lack of faith, unbelief, or doubt

ii) Not spending time in the Word

iii) Wrong teaching

iv) Lack of patience. Sometimes God has not spoken yet and all we need to do is wait.

v) Too busy/ Not listening (Psalm 46:10)

vi) Our minds are already made up

vii) Living in sin—Sin deadens people to hearing God

Conclusion

Whenever God speaks to us, and we know that we know that He has, it doesn't always mean that thing will come to pass with no trouble or resistance. Sometimes you hear God, but the other person involved did not hear Him. This could hinder the results and manifestation of what God wants to do.

I will give you a simple life experience: One time, God spoke to me, and I took some steps in the direction of getting a job God had placed on my heart. Actually, before that, I had been approached about the upcoming job. It was a part-time job, and I was working full-time in a different role. I prayed, and I believe that the Lord was leading me in the direction of taking that new position even though it was part-time at that time. I took some steps to get this job but didn't get it. God had spoken to me, and I fully knew it, but it never materialized. I still believe I heard God correctly even as I write this but it never happened.

The point of this is that when God speaks to you, it doesn't always or auto-matically come to pass, especially if there are other parties or people involved. God's Word and will are dependent on other people to come to pass even after you have heard God clearly.

Chapter Fourteen

What Is the Baptism of the Holy Spirit?

"Now when the apostles which were at Jerusalem heard that Samaria had received the word of God, they sent unto them Peter and John: Who, when they were come down, prayed for them, that they might receive the Holy Ghost: (For as yet he was fallen upon none of them: only they were baptized in the name of the Lord Jesus.) Then laid they their hands on them, and they received the Holy Ghost."

—Acts 8:14-17

In simple terms, **the baptism of the Holy Spirit is an experience after salvation in which a born-again believer receives or is filled or baptized in the Holy Spirit**. Being born again and being baptized in the Holy Ghost are separate experiences. It's true that when one gets born again, he has the Holy Spirit but that's just a partial truth.

When someone is born again, The Holy Spirit is **IN** them (John 14:17), but when they get filled with the Holy Ghost, the Holy Spirit is **UPON** them (Acts 1:5,8) and flows out of them causing and empowering them to be a witness. There is more to the Holy Spirit than the initial experience when we get born again, and I dare say that there is even more after one is baptized in the Holy Spirit hence Ephesians 5:18. With that said, we should be experiencing the power of the Holy Spirit in the present day. We should be having better and bigger experiences than the initial experience of the Holy Ghost infilling. The initial experience was great but there is more, and we should not be caught up with just that. We do not want our greatest experience with God and the baptism in the Holy Spirit to be behind us. It should be today.

The new believer already has the Holy Spirit living in them but this time the Holy Spirit comes upon them, or they are immersed in Him who empowers them to be witnesses of the Lord Jesus and to live a victorious Christian life.

The other way I love to say this is that when you get saved, you get the Holy Spirit but when you get baptized in the Holy Spirit, the Holy Spirit gets you. Your life is led by and yielded to the control of the Holy Spirit. Take an example of a drunkard who is influenced by alcohol, in this case, the believer is influenced by the Holy Spirit unto the good and godly. Another way to say this is that when you get saved you receive the Holy Spirit but the filling to overflow happens when you get filled with the Holy Spirit. It's like another dose of the Holy Spirit that makes one overflow.

In Acts 8:12-17, Phillip preached Christ to the Samaritans because they weren't born again yet. He did not preach the Holy Ghost to them. The world (sinners) cannot receive the Holy Spirit according to John 14:16-17. The Holy Spirit is God's gift to believers–His children (Luke 11:13), not the sinners. Jesus is God's gift to the world (John 3:16). Anyone that receives this Holy Spirit must be a believer. An unbeliever cannot receive the baptism of the Holy Spirit. Receiving the Holy Spirit with the evidence of speaking in tongues could be a simultaneous experience with salvation, or it could be a separate experience, but it doesn't happen before one is born again. Simply put, baptism in the Holy Spirit is a separate experience to being born again.

We see clearly that the Samaritans were born again (having received the Word of God), YET Peter and John prayed for them to receive the Holy Ghost. This makes it clear that they had not been filled or baptized in the Holy Spirit at the New birth. **Although every believer has the Holy Spirit on the inside of them, not every believer is filled or baptized in the Holy Ghost.** This was and is a separate experience to being born again as we see Peter and John coming to pray for them.

The Holy Spirit is the main Agent that works on a person to be born again.

    a) He draws us to the Lord.

    b) Baptizes us into the body of Christ (1 Corinthians 12:3).

    c) Creates a new Spirit on the inside of us.

    d) Witnesses to our spirit that we are children of God.

After all the above, we then move in to be filled and baptized in Him by the Lord Jesus performing the baptism.

We see this also in Acts 9 in regard to Paul's story. Paul got saved when Jesus appeared to him. When Ananias came to him, it was not to pray for his salvation but to have him filled with the Holy Ghost. Paul was already a "brother" according to Ananias. If Paul already had the Holy Spirit at the New birth, which he did, and there was nothing more, then the Lord would not have sent Ananias for him to be baptized in the Holy Spirit. This simply shows that being born again and being filled with the Holy Spirit are a separate experience from the initial salvation experience.

John 20:22 says, *"And when he had said this, he breathed on them, and saith unto them, Receive ye the Holy Ghost:"* Notice that the disciples received the Holy Spirit, but a few days later were actually baptized in the Holy Spirit. Acts 2:4 says, *"And they were all filled with the Holy Ghost, and began to speak with other tongues, as the Spirit gave them utterance."*

There is a lot of confusion when it comes to speaking in tongues. Some people think that the Holy Spirit will open their mouth and cause them to speak in tongues. Acts 2:4 clearly says that **the people did the speaking** while the Holy Spirit gave them utterance. Who did the speaking? The people did. Who gave the utterance? The Holy Spirit. For one to speak in tongues, they will have to **yield** to the Holy Spirit and cooperate with Him.

Every time the Holy Ghost falls on a believer in the NT, a gift of the Holy Spirit manifests and gives evidence that they have received that infilling of the spirit. Usually, they spoke in tongues, magnified God, or prophesied.

a) They spoke in new tongues

b) They magnified God

c) They prophesied

"While Peter yet spake these words, the Holy Ghost fell on all them which heard the word. And they of the circumcision which believed were astonished, as many as came with Peter, because that on the Gentiles also was poured out the gift of the Holy Ghost. For they heard them speak with tongues, and magnify God."

—Acts 10:44-46

So, Peter:

a) Spoke with tongues

b) Magnified God

"He said unto them, Have ye received the Holy Ghost since ye believed? And they said unto him, We have not so much as heard whether there be any Holy Ghost. And he said unto them, Unto what then were ye baptized? And they said, Unto John's baptism. Then said Paul, John verily baptized with the baptism of repentance, saying unto the people, that they should believe on him which should come after him, that is, on Christ Jesus. When they heard this, they were baptized in the name of the Lord Jesus. And when Paul had laid his hands upon them, the Holy Ghost came on them; and they spake with tongues, and prophesied."

—Acts 19:2-6

Here we see that new believers:

a) Spoke with tongues

b) Prophesied

Speaking in tongues is a gift that follows the Baptism of the Holy Spirit (as the main evidence of that baptism), but it is possible to be baptized in the Holy Spirit and have the new language (tongues) come in later or not speak in tongues immediately. Speaking in tongues or praying in the spirit is the normal manifestation and is available to all who are baptized in the spirit, although not all believers step out in faith and release this gift. Prophecy is another manifestation mentioned in Scripture. The heavenly prayer language (speaking in tongues) exists in every believer who has asked to be filled with the Holy Spirit (Matthew 7:11; Luke 11:10-13). **It's just a matter of releasing it.** Like I said earlier, when you get born again, you get the Holy Spirit but when you get baptized in the Holy Spirit, the Holy Spirit "gets" you. To have a powerful victorious Christian life, a believer needs to be filled with the Holy Spirit.

> *"For every one that asketh receiveth; and he that seeketh findeth; and to him that knocketh it shall be opened. If a son shall ask bread of any of you that is a father, will he give him a stone? or if he ask a fish, will he for a fish give him a serpent? Or if he shall ask an egg, will he offer him a scorpion? If ye then, being evil, know how to give good gifts unto your children: how much more shall your heavenly Father give the **Holy Spirit** to them that ask him?"*
>
> *–Luke 11:10-13 (emphasis mine)*

AND Matthew 7:11: *"If ye then, being evil, know how to give good gifts unto your children, how much more shall your Father which is in heaven give **good things** to them that ask him?"*

Luke 11:10-13 and Matthew 7:11 use the **Holy Spirit and good things interchangeably**. The Holy Spirit is a good thing for all of us.

A. **There are three types of Baptisms we find in scripture; knowing who is doing the baptism and the object being baptized into is very critical to understanding these types of Baptisms.**

   a) Baptism in the body of Christ happens when you get born again

      i) This is done by the Holy Spirit–1 Cor 12:13.

    b) Baptism in the Holy Spirit. When the Holy Ghost "gets" you (Acts 1 and 2)

        i)   This is done by Jesus, see Matthew 3:11; Luke 3:16; and Mark 1:8.

    c) Water baptism

        a)   This is done by a believer or minister.

B. Terms used to describe or define the baptism of the born-again believer into the spirit:

    a) The promise of the Father–Luke 24:49, Acts 1:4, Acts 2:39.

    b) Being endued with power–Luke 24:29.

    c) Receiving power–Acts 1:8.

    d) Being baptized in or with the Holy Spirit–Acts 1:5.

    e) Being filled with the spirit–Acts 4:31.

    f) Receiving the Holy Spirit–Acts 8:15-17.

    g) Having the Holy Spirit fall on you–Acts 11:44.

    h) Having the Holy Spirit come upon you–Acts 19:6.

C. Who needs it?

All believers need the baptism of the Holy Spirit. It is critical to remember that it is not a requirement for salvation. It is beneficial for this life but not the afterlife. **The baptism of the Holy Ghost with the evidence of speaking in tongues is very beneficial to a born-again believer.**

1 Corinthians 14:39 tells us, *"Wherefore, brethren, covet to prophesy, and forbid not to speak with tongues."* Many people have done a good job to stop people and discourage them from speaking in tongues, but the Bible is very clear. It says, **FORBID NOT** to speak in tongues.

a) Acts 2:38-39 says that the promise of the Holy Ghost is for **all believers** now and those that are to come.

b) *"So that ye come behind in **no gift**; waiting for the coming of our Lord Jesus Christ:"* –1 Corinthians 1:7 (emphasis mine)

c) *"And be not drunk with wine, wherein is excess; **but be filled with the Spirit**;"* –Ephesians 5:18 (emphasis mine)

   i) The Word of God admonishes us to be filled with the Holy Spirit instead of being drunk with wine.

D. First, I want to establish that there are two main classifications of tongues:

a) The gift of speaking in tongues (1 Corinthians 12:7, 10, 11; 14:2, 4, 5, 18-19)

   i) This is a type of tongues that each believer receives and speaks in after he or she is filled or baptized in the Holy Spirit. It is also referred to as a prayer language. It is given to every man, not just some.

   ii) While speaking in this type of tongues, we speak unto God not unto men. It doesn't have to be interpreted. It is for personal edification, not the church. No man understands this type of tongues.

b) The ministry gift of tongues (1 Corinthians 12:28-30).

   i) This type of tongues operates in a church service and must be interpreted to the edification of the church. It is given primarily for the church body through a person that operates in this office or ministry gift of tongues. It is given to **some** not all (1 Corinthians 12:28). With this type of ministry or office gift of tongues, God is speaking to man, therefore it must be interpreted so that people understand what is being spoken by God through this ministry gift of tongues.

ii) There is a difference between the ministry gift of tongues given as a gift to the church and the gift of speaking in tongues given to the individual.

The benefits of the gift of speaking in tongues (prayer language)

A. Our spirit prays which is a supernatural way of communicating with God

a) *"For if I pray in an unknown tongue, **my spirit prayeth**, but my understanding is unfruitful. What is it then? I will pray with the spirit, and I will pray with the understanding also: I will sing with the spirit, and I will sing with the understanding also."* –1 Corinthians 14:14-15 (emphasis mine)

i) Did you know that your born-again spirit can pray?

ii) When we pray in tongues (in the spirit), our spirit prays and bypasses the fears and doubts of our minds. When you pray in tongues, it is your spirit that's praying not your mind. When you pray in English or a known language to you, it is not your spirit praying but your soul (mind). Your mind isn't involved while praying in the spirit, but your spirit is. This is an adult conversation with God because our Spirit is the mature and complete part of us.

iii) **Speaking in tongues is a supernatural way of communicating with God.** We all have a natural way but there is also a supernatural way.

iv) We do not have to struggle to come up with words to say all the time. We can simply switch to speaking in tongues and bypass our ignorance and fears in a known language.

B. We speak unto God

1 Corinthians 14:2, *"For he that speaketh in an unknown tongue speaketh not unto men, but unto God: for no man understandeth him; howbeit in the spirit he speaketh mysteries."*

a) When we speak in tongues, we speak unto God not unto man. No one understands us–this includes the devil.

    i) By speaking in tongues, we are praying out God's perfect will.

b) God has given us a supernatural and divine means by which we can speak to Him. In the spirit we speak divine secrets hence we aren't being understood by men. Secrets can't be understood until revealed.

C. Clarity of God's Word, more revelation outflow, and sensitivity to God

a) Example: One day I was at my house and I was prompted to start praying in tongues. I later called my wife and asked if she was okay. She told me that as she was driving on the highway, her tire exploded. Praise God she did not crash. She was saved from any form of accident and walked away safe and sound. But the key point is that when I asked her what time this incident occurred, I realized it was the exact time I was praying in tongues. Hallelujah! As I prayed in the spirit, God took those prayers in tongues and applied them to protect her life.

b) Speaking in tongues increases your ability to hear from God and be led by Him. Why? Because as you speak in tongues, you speak the mysteries of God (1 Corinthians14:2) and if you pray to interpret (1 Corinthians14:13), the Holy Spirit will reveal things to you because when you pray in tongues, you are speaking and praying the wisdom and mysteries of God.

c) Scriptural hunger and desire for things of God. Speaking in tongues makes you hungrier for God and the things of God and less drawn to the things of the world. This happens best through a continual experience not just the initial evidence of the baptism of the Holy Spirit.

d) Speaking in tongues or praying in the Spirit keeps us in the Spirit and our eyes set on the Spirit rather than the flesh. If you want to reap the greatest benefits of the baptism of the Holy Spirit with the evidence of speaking in tongues, you need to make an effort to maintain a Spirit-filled led life by praying MUCH in other tongues. Pray much in tongues (1 Corinthians 14:28).

    i) Keeps us conscious of God's presence. Believers act in the flesh because they aren't conscious of God's presence.

    ii) Because we are in tune with the things of God and are conscious of Him, praying in tongues will protect us from the contamination of the world as the junk around you will not register or record in your soul as you speak in tongues.

e) Speaking in tongues waters our gift, not another man's gift. If you are a teacher, it will water teaching and if you are a prophet it will water the prophetic in you.

    i) My personal experience from the time I got filled with the Holy Spirit and started speaking in new tongues was that I started to receive more revelation from God's Word like never before. I started to receive a better understanding and insight in the Word of God. In addition to that, I started receiving promptings from the Holy Spirit and in many cases revealing to me things to come. It's amazing and I'm enjoying it.

f) Praying in tongues is an introduction to the gifts of the Spirit mentioned in 1 Corinthians 12. One of the reasons for this is that speaking in tongues increases our sensitivity to the things of God and the Spirit and keeps us God conscious hence being easy to be led by Him. Speaking in tongues is a supernatural doorway into the supernatural realm of God.

D. Supplication for others and the unknown

*"Praying always with all prayer and **supplication in the Spirit**, and watching thereunto with all perseverance and **supplication for all saints**."*
                           –Ephesians 6:18 *(emphasis mine)*

a) Supplication in the Spirit is referring to speaking or praying in tongues. 1 Corinthians 14:2 *For he that speaketh in an unknown tongue speaketh not unto men, but unto God: for no man understandeth him; howbeit **in the spirit** he speaketh mysteries.*

   i) Notice that in 1 Corinthians 14:2, *"in the spirit"* is used which clearly is referring to speaking in tongues as used in Ephesians 6:18.

   ii) When we put these verses together we conclude that **IN THE SPIRIT** is referring to speaking in tongues. In other words, supplication for all the saints can only be done and achieved **in the spirit**–praying in tongues (1 Corinthians 14:2).

   • Supplication in spirit helps us to effectively supplicate for All the saints. To pray for all the saints, we do that by praying in the spirit– praying in tongues.

   • In our natural mind, we do not know all things, but in our spirit we do. We can pray for all the saints in the spirit.

b) How do you pray for all the saints? How do you pray for what you don't know in your natural mind? How do you pray for someone who needs prayer that you know not what you should pray for? When you speak in tongues, you pray wisdom, the will of God, and your prayers cannot miss. You also pray for what things you do not know whereas in the natural mind you pray for things that you know. We can pray for all the saints in the spirit. This is impossible to do in the natural mind or a known language. We can only do that by praying in the spirit– praying in tongues.

c) One of the main benefits of speaking in tongues is that we get to pray for what our natural mind does not know. In the spirit, we are able to pray for things to come before they ever happen as we will sense in our spirit what we are praying about. When we pray in a known language, we pray for what we already do know but we can't pray for what we do not know. Speaking in tongues helps us achieve that. How powerful! Hallelujah!

E. Build yourself up in your most Holy Faith and keep yourself in the love of God

a) *"But ye, beloved, building up yourselves on your most holy faith, praying in the Holy Ghost, Keep yourselves in the love of God, looking for the mercy of our Lord Jesus Christ unto eternal life."* –Jude 20:20-21

    i) When we pray in the spirit, we build ourselves up in our most Holy faith and we keep ourselves in the love of God. This shows how powerful and critical praying in tongues is.

    ii) Our faith is stirred up as we pray in tongues. Faith is built to the greatest and holiest level when we pray in the Holy Spirit.

F. Keeps us in the love of God

a) *"But ye, beloved, building up yourselves on your most holy faith, praying in the Holy Ghost, Keep yourselves in the love of God, looking for the mercy of our Lord Jesus Christ unto eternal life." –Jude 20:20-21*

    i) When we pray in the spirit, we build ourselves up in our most Holy faith and **we keep ourselves in the love of God**.

    ii) This indicates that we can leave or depart from the love of God. We keep ourselves in the love of God and receive revelation of His love by praying in the spirit (tongues).

G. Personal edification

a) *"He that speaketh in an unknown tongue edifieth himself; but he that prophesieth edifieth the church."* –1 Corinthians 14:4

    i) The word "edification" comes from a Greek word that means "to be a house builder" (Strong's Concordance). When we speak in tongues, we build ourselves up like a house is built. We lay a foundation that helps the house become firm and emboldened.

ii) Very few things that we do build us up; one of them is speaking in tongues or praying in spirit.

iii) The purpose of tongues or our prayer language has been abused by some. They are meant for our personal spiritual edification (1 Corinthians 14:4) and communication to God.

- A public speaking in tongues in the same way as one who would be teaching must be interpreted to edify the rest of the body (1 Corinthians 14:27-28).
- Tongues can be spoken in public if the whole body is praying in tongues, not from the pulpit speaking or teaching the Word.

H. True worship

a) John 4:24 says, *"God is a Spirit: and they that worship him must worship him in spirit and in truth."*

i) The highest level of worship and communion with God is the one that flows from our spirit, not the physical or emotional realm. Because God is a Spirit, the best form of worship is spirit to Spirit worship.

ii) Praying in the Spirit falls under the same category as spirit to Spirit worship and communion with God.

iii) When we speak in tongues our spirit prays (1 Corinthians 14:14), directly to God who is also a Spirit. Praying or speaking in tongues is a spirit to Spirit communication very unique, supernatural, and powerful.

I. Intercession

a) *"Likewise, the Spirit also helpeth our infirmities: for we know not what we should pray for as we ought: but the Spirit itself maketh intercession for us with groanings which cannot be uttered. And he that searcheth the hearts knoweth what is the mind of the Spirit, because he maketh intercession for the saints according to the will of God." –Romans 8:26-27*

    i) Praying in tongues is the highest level of intercession. Whenever we speak in tongues, we allow the Holy Spirit to intercede for us on a greater level.

J. Blessing and giving thanks well to God

Have you ever thought or felt like you wanted to praise God but never found the exact words for expression? I have had moments when I wanted to praise God, but I could not find the exact words to express my praise and gratitude unto the Lord. No one can fully express how thankful they are to God in a natural language. Tongues help us accomplish that. The best way to give thanks is by speaking in tongues because we do thanksgiving well through this means.

    a) 1 Cor 14:16-17 says, *"Else when thou shalt **bless with the spirit**, how shall he that occupieth the room of the unlearned say Amen at **thy giving of thanks**, seeing he understandeth not what thou sayest? For thou verily **givest thanks well**, but the other is not edified."*

        i) The context of these verses is speaking in tongues. Speaking in tongues is used interchangeably with **"bless with the spirit"**, and **"thy giving of thanks"**. These verses further say that praying or speaking in tongues is giving thanks–yet not just giving thanks but giving thanks well. If we want to give thanks well, look no further. We do so through speaking in tongues.

K. Magnifies and Glorifies God

To magnify means to make bigger and to lift up.

    a) Acts 10:46 says, *"For they heard them speak with tongues, and magnify God."*

i) Speaking in tongues glorifies and magnifies God.

ii) If we want to magnify and glorify God, we should flip the tongue switch and begin speaking in tongues.

L. Boldness

"And now, Lord, behold their threatenings: and grant unto thy servants, that with all boldness they may speak thy word, By stretching forth thine hand to heal; and that signs and wonders may be done by the name of thy holy child Jesus. And when they had prayed, the place was shaken where they were assembled together; and they were all filled with the Holy Ghost, and they spake the word of God with boldness. And the multitude of them that believed were of one heart and of one soul: neither said any of them that ought of the things which he possessed was his own; but they had all things common. And with great power gave the apostles witness of the resurrection of the Lord Jesus: and great grace was upon them all."

–Acts 4:29-33

Notice they were **all** filled–not some. Even then, this is was after they had prayed. Prayer was key for them being filled and the place being shaken.

After they were filled, having been filled earlier in Acts 2, they were filled again, and a few notable things were seen:

a) They spoke the Word with **boldness.** This implies that they were not bold before but after they were filled with the Holy Ghost. This was another level or dimension of boldness. Being filled with the Holy Spirit and speaking in tongues will cause boldness to spring out of you hence leading to salvations.

i) The disciples that had fled from the Lord (Matthew 26:56; Mark 14:50) in terror were now different men (1 Samuel 10:6) after they were filled with the Holy Ghost.

ii) Example: After Peter got filled with the Holy Spirit, he was no longer the same man. Before this filling of the Holy Spirit, Peter was fearful and denied the Lord. However, after the baptism of the Holy Spirit, he became as bold as a lion, standing up and preaching the gospel and getting over 3000 people saved (**Acts 2:14-41**). He later died the death of a martyr. This was another Peter. He had been turned into another man for sure as King Saul was at the beginning of his reign (1 Samuel 10:6).

"And the Spirit of the LORD will come upon thee, and thou shalt prophesy with them, and shalt be turned into another man." –1 Samuel 10:6

   iii) You can't speak with boldness what you do not know. These men and women knew the Word.

   iv) Notice also that whenever they were filled with the Holy Spirit, they spoke either the Word of God or new tongues. You can't separate being filled with speaking!

b) Great power

Because of them being filled with the Holy Spirit, they were given great power.

c) Great grace

Yet not just great power alone, but also great grace. All these were results of all of them being filled with the Holy Spirit.

Notice also that there is not just one filling (Acts 2). Acts 4:31 shows that there was another filling of all the disciples. Furthermore, Ephesians 5:18 tells us to be being filled which indicates a continuous process. When were you last filled? In our souls, we need a continuous filling. Unlike our born-again spirits, our souls leak, hence the need for a continuous filling of the Holy Spirit.

M. Brings refreshing and rest

a) *"In the law it is written, with men of other tongues and other lips will I speak unto this people; and yet for all that will they not hear me, saith the Lord."* –1 Corinthians 14:21

"For with stammering lips and another tongue will he speak to this people. To whom he said, **this is the rest wherewith ye may cause the weary to rest; and this is the refreshing: yet they would not hear.**" –Isaiah 28:11:12 (emphasis mine)

  i) Paul quoted this OT verse in relation to speaking in tongues. A closer look at the verse he quoted reveals more detail that speaking in tongues releases refreshing and rest. Are you weary and in need of a rest or refreshing? Speaking in tongues will get you the rest and refreshing you need. As you begin to speak and pray in tongues, your spirit releases strength and refreshment into your soul.

  ii) Some things get cured simply by rest and refreshing ourselves. Sometimes all it takes for us to be fully healed is to get a bedrest. We can achieve this rest or bedrest by speaking in tongues. This is the best means to rest ever.

Holy Ghost Baptism Before Special Assignment

Anyone who had a calling from the Lord for a special assignment or was called to preach got baptized in the Holy Ghost, Above all, if Jesus did, we all need to as well! If Jesus needed to operate in the power of the Holy Ghost, we should too.

a) Paul was baptized in the Holy Spirit (Acts 9:10-17). Paul spoke in tongues (1 Corinthians 14:18).

b) Jesus was baptized in the Holy Ghost (Acts 10:38). If Jesus needed the baptism of the Holy Spirit, who are we not to need it.

c) Peter was too (Acts 2, Acts 4:31).

d) John the Baptist was baptized in the Holy Spirit from his mother's womb (Luke 1:15).

Interpret

When you speak or pray in tongues, pray with expectation and pray to interpret (1 Corinthians 14:13). Interpreting means that your understanding becomes fruitful OR it yields fruit in that you begin to understand what you were praying in the spirit, see things clearly, have revelation knowledge, have a change of attitude, and get a different perspective.

Conclusion

One of the most important things we can do when we come up against a difficult situation is to pray in tongues. Speaking in tongues is like flipping a supernatural switch. We turn on a powerful generator and the life and wisdom of God that is in our spirit starts coming out of our mouth.

In your spirit is where your new life is, it's where the power of God in us dwells. We aren't just natural beings; we are natural as well as spiritual beings. Speaking or praying in tongues is essential in releasing what is in our new, born-again spirit. Speaking in tongues empowers us to discern and follow God's will.

Chapter Fifteen

What Are Some of the Objections to Speaking in Tongues?

There are multiple objections that many people give to speaking in tongues—some sincere, some not! Before I list them, I want to point out that the baptism in the Holy Spirit with the evidence of speaking in tongues is well established in the scripture.

Five recorded instances in the New Covenant of people speaking in tongues.

a) Day of Pentecost (Initial filling)–Acts 2:1-4.

b) The Samaritans Philip preached to–Acts 8:5-8, 12, 14-17. Peter and John were sent down to minister the baptism of the Holy Spirit to them.

c) Paul, then Saul of Tarsus–Acts 9:4-6, 10-12, 17-18. This was done by a "certain disciple, Ananias." He wasn't one of the twelve Apostles.

d) Cornelius and His household–Acts 10:13-15, 44-46. These were not laid hands on. The Holy Spirit fell upon them without laying on of hands.

e) Disciples at Ephesus–Acts 19:1-6. This was done by Paul.

f) Finally, Ephesians 5:18 encourages to be being filled by the Spirit which shows that this is not just a one time thing.

A. Jesus did not speak in tongues.

It's clear that Jesus never spoke in tongues nor the interpretation of it. Why then should the believer, right? Although it is true that Jesus did not speak in tongues, He was baptized in the Holy Spirit and so was John the Baptist.

First, it is crucial to understand that the speaking in tongues specifically was a gift that was promised after the coming of the Holy Spirit during the dispensation or age of the church and the Holy Spirit. The disciples also did not speak in tongues until after the Holy Spirit was poured out (Acts 2), although they operated in all the other supernatural gifts during the earthly ministry of Jesus. We do find all the seven supernatural gifts in 1 Corinthians 12 manifested in the life of Jesus but not the speaking in tongues and the interpretation of tongues.

These two supernatural gifts (tongues and the interpretation of tongues) are distinctive and specific to the New Covenant under the Holy Spirit Dispensation or the church age which started on the day of Pentecost. When the Holy Spirit was poured out or His dispensation was beginning, Jesus was already gone. He had checked out. (Acts 1:9-11). He did not have the time nor was He around when the Holy Spirit was being poured out or He would have spoken in tongues during the Holy Spirit dispensation.

Furthermore, He made it clear that believers would speak in new tongues in Mark 16:16-18. Not a few but all. People could only be born again after His resurrection and shortly after which the Holy Spirit was poured out marking the dispensation of the Holy Spirit and the church age.

These new tongues were for believers. Technically speaking, Jesus was not a believer nor was John the Baptist. Jesus was not even under the New Covenant. The New Covenant started after He resurrected and ascended into heaven and the Holy Spirit was poured out.

In Mark 16, all the five signs are supernatural gifts that the Lord spoke about although some have attempted to explain away tongues as not using vulgar words or dirty jokes.

B. Speaking in tongues is of the devil.

The devil has fought speaking in tongues because he knows it's powerful. Religious people will sometimes say speaking in tongues is "of the devil". But if speaking in tongues is of the devil, why can't you go to the bar or a strip club and hear or find people there speaking in tongues? Why don't evil people or criminals speak or pray in tongues? It is an argument that doesn't even make sense.

If speaking in tongues is of the devil, then we all should have spoken in tongues and magnified God in the world before we got born again. We wouldn't have to be born again to be speaking in tongues if that were the case.

Because of the power of the baptism of the Holy Spirit with evidence of speaking in tongues, the devil has been working day and night to discredit it and even talk people out of it. However, the Bible teaches that we should *"Forbid not to speak in tongues"* (1 Corinthians 12:39). The man that wrote three-quarters of the New Covenant spoke in tongues more than all of them (1 Corinthians 14:18). There is something to that.

Do you have to speak in tongues? You don't have to speak in tongues, you get to speak in tongues! It isn't a requirement to get saved, it is just a benefit. The Scriptures do not only teach *speaking* in tongues, but also speaks of singing in tongues (1 Corinthians 14:15). Those that oppose it, would have to oppose both.

a) *"Now when they heard this, they were pricked in their heart, and said unto Peter and to the rest of the apostles, Men and brethren, what shall we do? Then Peter said unto them, Repent, and be baptized every one of you in the name of Jesus Christ for the remission of sins, and ye shall receive the gift of the Holy Ghost. For the promise is unto you, and to your children, and to all that are afar off, even as many as the LORD our God shall call."* – Acts 2:37-39

   i) The gift of the Holy Spirit including the speaking in tongues was a promise to all believers and all that will believe in the future.

b) *"And these signs shall follow them that believe; In my name shall they cast out devils; **they shall speak with new tongues.**"* – Mark 16:17 (emphasis mine)

i) Jesus promised that those who believe in Him shall speak with new tongues. If speaking in tongues were of the devil, then why did Jesus promise it to the believers? He would have promised it to the unbelievers, not the believers.

c) *"For they heard them speak with tongues, and **magnify God**. Then answered Peter,"* – Acts 10:46 (emphasis mine).

i) Speaking in tongues magnifies God, not the devil. Something of the devil doesn't glorify or magnify God at the same time.

e) *"For everyone that asketh receiveth; and he that seeketh findeth; and to him that knocketh it shall be opened. If a son shall ask bread of any of you that is a father, will he give him a stone? or if he ask a fish, will he for a fish give him a serpent? Or if he shall ask an egg, will he offer him a scorpion? If ye then, being evil, know how to give good gifts unto your children: how much more shall your heavenly Father give the Holy Spirit to them that ask him?"* –Luke 11:10-13 (emphasis mine)

"If ye then, being evil, know how to give good gifts unto your children, how much more shall your Father which is in heaven give good things to them that ask him?" –Matthew 7:11

Luke 11:10-13 and Matthew 7:11 use the **Holy Spirit and good things interchangeably**, which means the Holy Spirit is a good thing for all of us. Why would we not want a good thing, much more from God?

The head

Speaking in tongues is spiritual, your natural brain will not get it and it will sound silly to your brain. **It takes faith to pray in tongues just as it takes faith to be saved, healed, delivered, prospered, etc. If you don't step out in faith, you will never pray in tongues.** You do it by and through faith.

Similarly, one of the main reasons why many people don't receive the Lord as their Savior is because they are trying to reason it out with their heads. It doesn't make much sense in the beginning. They are so in tune with the natural world they ignore the existence of the spiritual world which created the visible things of the world.

They are trying to believe with their heads and not with their hearts and it never works. The Bible says with the heart believing is made unto righteousness (Romans 10:9-10, Acts 8:37), not with the head. With our heart we have to believe that "God hath raised him from the dead, thou shalt be saved."

God's Word is written to or for your heart first, then your head next. If you can't get it with your heart, you can't get it with your head (1 Cor 2:14). The most difficult people to get to receive are often the very educated ones in the things of this world. It takes a lot to reach them, because everything to them is reasoning. Although reasoning is accepted and welcomed in the things of God, it can easily be a barrier to relationship with the Lord and understanding spiritual things of God.

If you pray in tongues for more than five minutes, your mind is going to say, "this is silly, what am I doing?" The carnal part of you will rise and try to get you back into the natural realm where it feels comfortable. You must make a decision to continue speaking in tongues in spite of what your mind is saying and thinking. It's an act of faith. Acts of faith often seem silly to the natural man (1 Corinthians 2:14).

Wrong teaching and ignorance

You can't believe what you don't know; faith comes when knowledge is present. God's Word reveals His will and knowing His will gives us the faith to believe for the impossible–and see it come to pass. Knowledge of God's Word is power (Romans 10:17).

One of the main reasons that tongues have been neglected by the body of Christ is because of a lack of scriptural teaching of the scope and value of speaking in tongues. If people can truly know and understand the value of being baptized in the Holy Spirit with the evidence of speaking in tongues, they would want it.

a) It's of the devil

- Some say that speaking in tongues is of the devil. However, on many occasions, Peter, Paul, and Jesus prayed for people to be baptized in the Holy Ghost. Were they praying that the believers be baptized of the devil? God forbid!

b) Tarry in Jerusalem physically

- Most people have believed that they need to be literally in Jerusalem to get filled with the Holy Spirit because Jesus told His disciples to tarry in Jerusalem.

- The Holy Spirit has been poured out. This command was before He was poured out. Now, that He has, we do not to have to tarry at all–not even in Jerusalem. You can fly into Jerusalem for a visit but not for being filled with the Holy Spirit.

c) Only Apostles can pray for people to receive the baptism of the Holy Spirit with the evidence of speaking in tongues.

Some have used Acts 8:14-17 where the apostles John and Peter were sent down to pray for the believers to receive the Holy Ghost. Phillip had preached the Lord unto them and they got saved but did not minister the baptism of the Holy Spirit to them which later happened through Peter and John (Acts 8:14-17).

However, Acts 9 debunks that belief and teaching. After Saul of Tarsus was blinded by the light that came from heaven on the road to Damascus to persecute the believers, a certain disciple named **Ananias** received a vision from the Lord with instructions to go pray for Paul to receive his sight and also be baptized in the Holy Ghost. He went and did all that the Lord commanded him. The key point is that he was not an apostle. He was just a disciple. This clearly shows that not just the original apostles ought to be praying for people to be baptized in the Holy Spirit but rather any believer.

d) Tongues have ceased. They have passed away with the apostles

i) Some have believed and taught that the gifts of the Spirit, specifically the speaking in tongues and the interpretation of tongues, have passed away with the apostles. Acts 2:37-39 and Mark 16:17 teach the very opposite of that belief. The gifts have not passed away with the apostles. They are alive and well today.

ii) 1 Corinthians 13:8 is where most people go to make the argument that tongues have ceased and/or passed away with the Apostles. "Charity never faileth: but whether *there be* prophecies, they shall fail; whether *there be* tongues, they shall cease; whether *there be* knowledge, it shall vanish away."

- First this passage says they shall cease, future tense, not they have ceased. It says that same for prophecies and knowledge. All these things are in the future tense not in the past tense. Knowledge as we speak is only increasing. It has not ceased. Tongues have not ceased any more than prophecies have, or knowledge has vanished.

- Secondly, it would be best to read the whole context. 1 Corinthians 12:13 shows clearly that this is speaking of a time in the future when we shall see face to face rather than darkly through a glass.

Ask!

"If ye then, being evil, know how to give good gifts unto your children: how much more shall your heavenly Father give the Holy Spirit to them that ask him?"

–Luke 11:13

If we want the Holy Spirit, we should ask. In many cases believers were filled with the Holy Spirit before they asked. I remember I was filled with the Holy Spirit and started to speak in tongues without asking or having hands laid on me.

Open your mouth and start to talk

If you want to speak in tongues, you can't speak or talk in tongues with your mouth closed. I have seen this on many occasions where someone wants to speak but they keep their mouth closed. You must open your mouth and begin to release syllables and believing, by faith, that God is inspiring it.

You don't have to worry about what it sounds like. If you want to walk on water, you must "get out of the boat". It doesn't matter if it's calm or not. It is similar to receiving the inspiration for a song. We hear it on the inside, but it is up to us to take a pen and paper and write down the expression(s) we have. God doesn't force us to write, nor is it an automatic handwriting. So, it is with speaking in tongues. The inspiration of the spirit is within, and we provide the vocal cords, the tongue, the lips, and the will.

We can start and stop, speak as loudly or softly as we wish. The Spirit gives inspiration, but we control how much we want to release the tongues or heavenly language.

You may start out like a "baby" does with just a syllable, and over time your language becomes more solid and fluent. Just start speaking in tongues and don't quit.

This passage of scripture completes this very well. 1 Corinthians 14:39 Wherefore, brethren, covet to prophesy, and **forbid not to speak with tongues**.

Chapter Sixteen

Is Healing Part of the Redemption?

Most people do not know or believe that healing was part of Christ's atonement or redemption. They do not realize that Jesus provided for their healing and therefore do not exercise their faith to receive it. This is true for financial prosperity, deliverance, peace, long life, and so forth. You can't receive what you do not know was provided for you. Faith is a product of knowing God's Word, will, and promises (Romans 10:9-10). No Word equals no faith. Knowing that God took our sickness will give you confidence to receive from God. This is also foundational to receiving healing.

Once we get a revelation of Jesus bearing our sickness and diseases as well as our sins for us, through His atonement on the cross, receiving healing becomes no more difficult than receiving forgiveness of sins. It is the same sacrifice that paid the price for our healing and forgiveness of sins (Mark 2:9; Psalm 103:3; James 5:13-15). Jesus' atonement sacrifice covers the physical as well as the spiritual needs of man. Not either, or one of the two, but both spiritual and physical healing.

One of the reasons that some people have not received their physical healing yet is because they have not taken and received healing as they have received the forgiveness of their sins. If you were to go to the bank to borrow some money, your level of assurance and confidence would not be the same as one who goes to the bank to withdraw money from his own account. The level of confidence between the two is completely different. Healing, deliverance,

GOT QUESTIONS? Got Answers

financial prosperity, peace, and everything you need are already in your spiritual account (Ephesians 1:3; 2 Peter 1:3). Quit asking and wondering, just make the withdrawal. It's already there! A lack of confidence and assurance is a sign of a lack of awareness of what is in our accounts.

If Jesus never paid for our sickness and diseases, then it would have been wrong for Him to heal the sick and diseased. And to add to this, If Jesus did not pay for healing, you can't get it. You can only get what God has provided by grace.

While answering this question of *"Is healing part of the redemption?"*, my goal is to show you that physical healing was part of Christ's atonement and redemption package. When Jesus paid for sin, He paid for all the negative results of sin which includes shame, condemnation, sickness, and disease.

A. Physical Healing

"When the even was come, they brought unto him many that were possessed with devils: and he cast out the spirits with his word, and healed all that were sick: That it might be fulfilled which was spoken by Esaias the prophet, saying, Himself took our infirmities, and bare our sicknesses."

– Matthew 8:16-17

a) These verses in Matthew 8:16-17 were fulfilled and were quoted from Isaiah 53:4 which says, *"Surely he hath borne our griefs, and carried our sorrows: yet we did esteem him stricken, smitten of God, and afflicted."*

b) Notice that in Matthew 8:16-17, the Holy Spirit led Matthew to substitute **"griefs and sorrows"** for **"infirmities and sickness."** Isaiah 53:4 would then read like this **"Surely he hath borne our infirmities and carried our sickness: yet we did esteem him stricken, smitten of God, and afflicted.**

c) The very **root** of physical sickness and disease is **SIN**. When Jesus dealt with the root, He undoubtedly dealt with its fruit.

174

d) Healing is not just a new concept found in the New Covenant. It has its fingerprint all over the OT. Jeremiah and David knew of God's will to heal (Psalm 6:2; 103:3; Jeremiah 17:14). Malachi 4:2, says *"But unto you that fear my name shall **the Sun of righteousness arise with healing in his wings;** and ye shall go forth, and grow up as calves of the stall."* If we see physical healing present and evident all through the Old Testament, during the inferior covenant, why should we doubt physical healing in the New Testament and that God wants us well under the superior and better covenant (Hebrews 7:22; 8:6-7).

B. Forgiveness of sins and healing always go together.

These scriptures further prove that healing was paid for just as sin was. They are provided and promised alongside each other. We should not separate the two. As a matter of truth, sin and disease all come from the same person—Satan. When Jesus defeated and destroyed Satan (Colossians 2:15 and 1 John 3:8), He destroyed all the things that he brings against us including sin, sickness, and disease. Sin is paid for, healing is paid for, prosperity is paid for, deliverance is paid for—believe and receive.

Here are some of the scriptures that further make the point that healing is a part of the redemption:

a) *"Who forgiveth all thine iniquities; who healeth all thy diseases;"* –Psalm 103:3

 i) The benefits of the atonement are listed in this chapter. Just as a job has benefits, salvation has benefits to the believer. Physical healing and forgiveness of sins are two of them.

b) *"Whether is it easier to say to the sick of the palsy, Thy sins be forgiven thee; or to say, Arise, and take up thy bed, and walk?"* –Mark 2:9

 i) Notice that Jesus offered forgiveness of sins along with physical healing. On multiple occasions, Jesus offered the physical healing of diseases with forgiveness of sins which further proves that He saw both the same way.

c) *"Surely he hath borne our griefs, and carried our sorrows: yet we did esteem him stricken, smitten of God, and afflicted. But he was wounded for our transgressions, he was bruised for our iniquities: the chastisement of our peace was upon him; and with his stripes we are healed."* –Isaiah 53:4-5

    i) If you are saved, you should be healed and if you are healed, you should be saved. Sickness, disease, and sin have all been paid for by the death of Jesus on the cross. Healing is part of the benefits package of Christ's atonement.

    ii) Our attitude towards sickness should be the same as towards sin. A difference in the way some view sin and sickness could be the reason why some aren't healed.

    iii) The sacrifice of Jesus delivered us from both sin and sickness, from sin and all its fruit (such as disease and sickness), from sin and its entire penalty.

    iv) Sickness is to the body what sin is to the spirit. If God is not willing to heal you, He is not willing to forgive your sins. Therefore, NO MORE SIN, NO MORE SICKNESS.

d) *"Is any among you afflicted? let him pray. Is any merry? Let him sing psalms. Is any sick among you? Let him call for the elders of the church; and let them pray over him, anointing him with oil in the name of the Lord: And the prayer of faith shall save the sick, and the Lord shall raise him up; and if he have committed sins, they shall be forgiven him."* –James 5:13-15

This verse ties forgiveness of sins to physical healing. Why? Because Jesus paid for both at the same time within the same sacrifice and atonement.

C. Physical and spiritual healing

*"But he was wounded for our **transgressions**, he was bruised for our iniquities: the chastisement of our peace was upon him; and with his stripes we are **healed**."*

–Isaiah 53:4-5 (emphasis mine)

a) The wounding, bruising, and **chastisement** of Jesus purchased our peace. Our peace and healing were all purchased by Jesus. We now have peace with God because of Jesus.

b) By the stripes of Jesus, we were healed. He took our sickness, so we might have physical healing (1 Peter 2:24 and Matthew 8:16-17).

c) The word "healed" in this verse implies being "**cured and made whole**," physically and spiritually. When Jesus dealt with our sin nature and spiritual problem, He also dealt with the effects of that sin nature such as sickness, disease, etc.

e) The word *"peace"* comes from Hebrew word *"Shalome Shalome"* which means wholeness, welfare, soundness, wellness (physical and spiritual healing).

f) Because Jesus took our sin, we are healed by His stripes. **If He had not paid for our sin, we should not expect healing of our bodies.** Also notice that these verses do not say "we will be healed", BUT "we ARE healed". Present tense!

Most people easily accept the forgiveness or deliverance of sins but not the forgiveness, deliverance or healing of sickness and disease. God will not make us sin the same way He will not make us sick. Healing was a part of Christ's atonement. This should settle it forever. Believe, receive, and be healed in Jesus' name.

Chapter Seventeen

Is It Sin to Be Wealthy?

Many people in the church and outside the church have a problem with being wealthy. Many have taken a vow of poverty, but not me. I'm of African descent, Uganda to be specific and one thing I know about Africans, among many, is that they can run. They are the best at long distance races in most occasions and I believe one of the reasons they run this well is because they are running from poverty. Just kidding! All our very being hates poverty, sickness, suffering, pain, death and so forth. Some people have rejected all the rest such as death, suffering, pain, but have sadly embraced poverty or a hatred for wealth and riches. Financial prosperity among many is one of the things that attracts others to the gospel. Who wants a broke God? Who wants a God who lives under the bridge and eats out of the garbage? Who wants such a God who is in lack of everything we need?

The thinking that being rich is sin has mainly been a result of misinterpretation of Mark 10:23-25 which says, *"And Jesus looked round about, and saith unto his disciples, How hardly shall they that have riches enter into the kingdom of God! And the disciples were astonished at his words. But Jesus answereth again, and saith unto them, Children, how hard is it for them that trust in riches to enter into the kingdom of God! It is easier for a camel to go through the eye of a needle, than for a rich man to enter into the kingdom of God."*

If taken in context, Jesus was speaking to young man who was rich but had his riches as the god of his life. His trust was more in his riches than in God. His riches had taken the place of God in his life and so for that reason it would be impossible for this man to enter the kingdom of heaven.

> *"For ye know the grace of our Lord Jesus Christ, that, though he was rich, yet for your sakes he became poor, that ye through his poverty might be rich."*
>
> —2 Corinthians 8:9 (KJV)

This is another verse that many people use to say that we should not be rich but poor. Some try to say this verse is talking about spiritual poverty. However, when you study the context, you will see that it is talking about money, literally.

You can't sincerely read the Scriptures and conclude that riches are not of God. If riches were sinful, then God would never have given riches to the many people we read about in the Bible such as:

a) **Abraham**

    i) "And Abram was very rich in cattle, in silver, and in gold." —Genesis 13:2

    ii) *"And Abraham was old, and well stricken in age: and* **the LORD had blessed Abraham in all things."** —Genesis 24:1

        • Abraham was not blessed in some or a few things but in all things. God would not have done this if it weren't His will. In Ephesians 1:3, we see the Word promising us the same thing. Ephesians 1:3 says, *"Blessed be the God and Father of our Lord Jesus Christ, who hath blessed us with all spiritual blessings in heavenly places in Christ."*

b) **King Solomon**

    i) *"And I have also given thee that which thou hast not asked, both riches, and honour: so that there shall not be any among the kings like unto thee all thy days."* —1 Kings 3:13

ii) *"And the king made silver to be in Jerusalem as stones..."* –1 Kings 10:27

c) Isaac

i) *"Then Isaac sowed in that land, and received in the same year an hundredfold: and the LORD blessed him. And the man waxed great, and went forward, and grew until he became very great: For he had possession of flocks, and possession of herds, and great store of servants: and the Philistines envied him."* –Genesis 26:12-14

- These people did not envy Isaac for his poverty. The people envied him because he was very wealthy. Poor people hardly have any enemies. What is there to envy?

ii) ***"And Abimelech said unto Isaac, Go from us; for thou art much mightier than we."*** – Genesis 26:16

- Isaac, with his servants, family and wealth was greater and mightier than the entire nation of Abimelech.

d) David

i) *"And he died in a good old age, full of days, riches, and honor: and Solomon his son reigned in his stead."* –1 Chronicles 29:28

e) Heaven

i) *"And the building of the wall of it was of jasper: and the city was pure gold, like unto clear glass. And the foundations of the wall of the city were garnished with all manner of precious stones. The first foundation was jasper; the second, sapphire; the third, a chalcedony; the fourth, an emerald; The fifth, sardonyx; the sixth, sardius; the seventh, chrysolyte; the eighth, beryl; the ninth, a topaz; the tenth, a chrysoprasus; the eleventh, a jacinth; the twelfth, an amethyst. And the twelve gates were twelve pearls; every several gate was of one pearl: and the street of the city was pure gold, as it were transparent glass."* –Revelation 21:18-21

f) **Job**

    i) *"His substance also was seven thousand sheep, and three thousand camels, and five hundred yoke of oxen, and five hundred she asses, and a very great household; so that this man was the greatest of all the men of the east."* –Job 1:3

Conclusion

The Word of God is full of evidence that our God is not a broke and busted God. Creation shows that. The complexity of the human body is also very telling. No price could purchase any of that. The bottom line is you can be poor if you want. I'm not joining you on your temporary adventure.

If you do not like your wealth and money, if money is evil, then send it all to me and I will write more books and change the world for Jesus. Would you like my address? If you aren't willing to do this, then you know deep down in your heart that riches and wealth aren't bad nor evil. Money is just a medium that we use. It is neither good nor bad. It is what we use it for that is bad or good. You do not have to do away with your wealth. You can use it to advance the kingdom of God (Deuteronomy 8:18). You can have both God and wealth or money as long as wealth and money do not have you.

Chapter Eighteen

Why Do Bad Things Happen to Good People? Does God Allow, Ordain, or Cause Natural Disasters Such as Tsunamis, Earthquakes and Birth Defects?

Although I believe this is a wrong question to ask, this is a question that everyone on earth has asked or has thought at some point. They think, *"I thought so and so was a good person, but why did God allow or do this to them?"*

One day, when this question came up, I instead thought, **"Why do good things happen to bad people? If bad things happen to good people, then it is certainly true that good things happen to bad people."** This is a question that many do not ask.

Not every question that is asked is a correct question. I think the right question should be something like, **why do good things happen to good and bad people** (Matthew 5:45 That ye may be the children of your Father which is in heaven: for he maketh his sun to rise on the evil and on the good, and sendeth rain on the just and on the unjust.), **or why does Satan allow, cause, and bring bad things to good people?**

It is quite interesting how most people think. When something good happens, they do not give God the glory or the credit, but if something bad happens, God is to blame. This is so wrong.

For example when one plane ever crashes, it's like God, why? When hundreds and thousands of planes land safely no one credits God. So, they blame God for the bad and take credit for the good.

To most people, it has never crossed their minds that someone else could be behind all these tragedies and losses except God. The first thing they think is God is responsible.

How about I submit to you a stunning new thought yet not new all?

1. What if Satan is responsible?

2. The truth is those who blame God for the bad and evil that happens in the world and in their lives, **do not KNOW God**. If they only knew a little bit about God or if they were in relationship with Him, they would be shocked to realize how wrong they have been all their lives. God is a good God. He is not what many people out there have presented Him to be.

You may not have all the answers, but you must settle this in your hearts that **God is a good God and Satan is a bad devil**.

a) In the word **"good"** you can get the word **"God"** and in the word **"devil"**, you can get **"evil"**. If it is good and unselfish it's God, and if it's bad it's the devil (Satan).

b) We need to credit God for the good and credit Satan for the evil.

A. Satan is truly responsible

a) It's time we started crediting Satan for all the evil he does and crediting God for all the good He does.

b) God does only good. Psalm 119:68 says, **"Thou art good, and doest good; teach me thy statutes."** That's His nature. He is a good God.

c) *"The thief cometh not, but for to steal, and to kill, and to destroy: I am come that they might have life, and that they might have it more abundantly."* –John 10:10

i) These scriptures are so clear. God came to give us **life and give it to us abundantly**. He did not come to take life.

ii) On the other side, Satan came to **steal, kill, and destroy**. It's that plain and simple.

B. A study of the life of Jesus:

a) No one can sincerely study the life of Jesus (Acts 10:38) and conclude that He did bad or evil. I don't care what your conclusions are, if they say otherwise, you are dead wrong.

b) According to John 8:29, Jesus did those things that were pleasing to the Father. Those things include healing and all the good things.

c) Jesus lived a life of love and destroyed the evil that Satan brought upon mankind during His earthly life and, eventually, died at the cross and was resurrected from the dead.

d) *"He that committeth sin is of the devil; for the devil sinneth from the beginning.* **"For this purpose the Son of God was manifested, that he might destroy the works of the devil."** –1 John 3:8 (emphasis mine)

    i) This verse clearly shows you that Jesus is not on the same side with the devil. He came to destroy the evil works of the devil such as sickness, sin, and all the plunder we see.

e) If He was the one who allowed all the sickness and the plunder of the enemy, **it would have been wrong for Him to heal the sick, cleanse the lepers, and raise the dead. He would have been doing that which is contrary to what He "allowed".**

f) The Bible also says that He was God manifest in the flesh (1 Timothy 3:16) which means His heart was to do good alone. The Scriptures also go on to say that He did the will of God.

    i) John 4:34: "Jesus saith unto them, My meat is to do the will of him that sent me, and to finish his work," which included healing the sick, cleansing the lepers, raising the dead and many more good things.

"For I have no pleasure in the death of him that dieth, saith the Lord God: wherefore turn yourselves, and live ye."

—Ezekiel 18:30-32; Ezekiel 33:11

C. God is not the one responsible, causing, nor allowing bad things such as sickness, disease, death, storms, birth defects, hunger, war, divorce, misery, you name it.

Some thoughts to remember in relation to why bad things happen.

1. **One on one**

    God's discipline of His children is **always one on one and always involves His Word, not a sickness, disease, natural disaster or tragedy** (Here are scriptures that show you how God teaches His children and it's all through His Word (2 Timothy 3:16-17; 1 Peter 2:2; 1 Corinthians 10:6-11; John 14:26; John 15:1-3; Joshua 1:8; Ephesians 4:11-13; Psalms 34:11; 94:12; 119:9-11,103,105,133).

    a) The Scriptures also teach clearly that the **Holy Spirit is the teacher–our Teacher**. He would teach us all things.

        i) The Holy Spirit teaches us, not tragedy or problems.

        ii) *"But the Comforter, which is the Holy Ghost, whom the Father will send in my name, he shall teach you all things, and bring all things to your remembrance, whatsoever I have said unto you."* –John 14:26

        iii) *"Howbeit when he, the Spirit of truth, is come, he will guide you into all truth: for he shall not speak of himself; but whatsoever he shall hear, that shall he speak: and he will show you things to come."* –John 16:13

        iv) *"But the anointing which ye have received of him abideth in you, and ye need not that any man teach you: but as the same anointing teacheth you of all things, and is truth, and is no lie, and even as it hath taught you, ye shall abide in him."* –1 John 2:27

2. **To save Lives, not destroy them**

"For the Son of man is not come to destroy men's lives, but to save them. And they went to another village."

–Luke 9:56

a) Jesus did not come to destroy lives but to save them. How would He die for the lives He destroyed? Satan is the true killer, stealer, and destroyer (John 10:10).

b) Those who think or even teach otherwise have missed the heart of God.

3. **Book of Revelation**

a) The book of Revelation describes a time in the future when God's judgment will rain upon unbelievers. However, today we are living in the age of grace where God is not imputing man's sins unto people (2 Corinthians 5:19, 21).

   i) *"And I beheld when he had opened the sixth seal, and, lo, there was a great earthquake; and the sun became black as sackcloth of hair, and the moon became as blood; And the stars of heaven fell unto the earth, even as a fig tree casteth her untimely figs, when she is shaken of a mighty wind. And the heaven departed as a scroll when it is rolled together; and every mountain and island were moved out of their places. And the kings of the earth, and the great men, and the rich men, and the chief captains, and the mighty men, and every bondman, and every free man, hid themselves in the dens and in the rocks of the mountains; And said to the mountains and rocks, Fall on us, and hide us from the face of him that sitteth on the throne, and from the wrath of the Lamb: For the great day of his wrath is come; and who shall be able to stand?"* –Revelation 6:12-17

b) If that was the judgment of God, it would be **more severe**, and it wouldn't be only in **selective places** or countries, but the entire world.

c) If it was God's judgment, it would be **very evident to all people** that it is God's judgment and people would not have to be told. They would just know it without explanation (Revelations 6:16). The fact that this has to be explained to people further proves that this is not the judgment of God.

    i) The judgement of God does not or will not have to be explained to people. It will be known by all intuitively.

4. **Tragedies happen to godly men and women, too.**

a) There is no doubt that when tragedies and bad things happen, godly men and women also lose their lives or suffer in such, but it is not God that killed them, allowed it to happen, nor is He judging them.

b) **God does not kill His own** (During Sodom and Gomorrah, God spared Lot and his family–Genesis 18:26, 28-32). God is a good God, and He will not destroy the righteous with the wicked. It is Satan that kills his own.

    i) One of the things holding back the wrath of God is the fact that the righteous are still present. The Lord will spare the entire city because of and for the sake of the righteous (Genesis 18:26, 28-32).

    ii) Abraham negotiated all the way starting from 50 to 45 to 40 to 30 to 20, and 10 people asking God if He would destroy a city that had the above number of righteous. God made it clear that he would not. God will not judge a city or country if His people are present.

5. **God created laws (spiritual and natural).**

a) When God created everything, He created laws of how things ought to operate. These laws would reward man if he followed them, but they would also destroy or punish man should he go against them.

b) We experience victory to the degree we cooperate with those laws.

i) Example: if a farmer does not plant a crop, he can't blame God for not receiving a harvest. It is the natural laws that punished him, not God.

c) God created laws but established punishments in these laws. **God is not the one that judges us, it is the laws that do that.**

i) When we violate gravity, it punishes us. When we violate fire, we get burnt, etc. Going against these laws releases punishment to us.

d) These laws are not partial. They do not work for only one sect of race, sex, or people.

i) Success is governed by laws and principles that are universal. Financial prosperity or a successful life is not determined by the place you live, but by your relationship with the Lord and knowing the laws that govern success.

D. Below, I list some of the reasons why bad things happen:

a) **Sin in general**

i) When God created all things, He did not create anything bad or evil. Everything was beautiful and good. After every day of creation, the Bible says, *"God saw that it was good"* (Genesis 1:25).

ii) Later on, God created man (Genesis 3) and gave him the commandment not to eat of the tree of the knowledge of good and evil, but when he did, his sin plunged the whole creation and human race into the problems we have today.

- Praise God for Jesus that He came and died for all our sins and restored us to the status God created us for, but sin in general corrupted the world and life.

- In general, it is the main reason why we see bad things happen or we see all the death, plunder, misery, sin, sickness, and destruction.

iii) The original sin in the garden committed by Adam and Eve **ushered in all these bad things**. None of all this mess existed until after the fall of man.

- Many times, we have done nothing so to speak, but because of this corruption that entered the world through sin, we tend to become unwilling partakers of the mess in the world.

iv) *"And as Jesus passed by, he saw a man which was blind from his birth. And his disciples asked him, saying, Master, who did sin, this man, or his parents, that he was born blind? Jesus answered, Neither hath this man sinned, nor his parents: but that the works of God should be made manifest in him."* –John 9:1-3

- In this verse, Jesus said neither the man nor the parents sinned for this man to be blind. It was sin in general that has caused this imperfection in this man from birth.
- Nonetheless, since He (Jesus) was now present, He was going to turn things around by destroying this blindness on this man's behalf thereby giving glory to God.
- He did not put blindness on this man, but because of His loving-kindness, he healed the man. Hallelujah!

b) **Man's free will**

This is a major factor in why bad things happen. Man has been given free will to choose his destiny. God has offered help in many ways, but He does not force us to make a choice nor does He make it for us.

i) *"I call heaven and earth to record this day against you, that I have set before you life and death, blessing and cursing: therefore choose life, that both thou and thy seed may live:"* –Deuteronomy 30:19

- Those who do not believe that they have free will will blame everyone else and will never take responsibility for anything.

c) **Fallen World**

This may come as a shock to some people, but this world is not heaven. It's the fallen world and things aren't going to be perfect like they are in heaven.

    i) *"These things I have spoken unto you, that in me ye might have peace. In the world ye shall have tribulation: but be of good cheer; I have overcome the world."* –John 16:33

    ii) Everything is not going be smooth in this world like it would be in heaven. You will have tribulation.

    iii) The world is the only hell a believer will ever experience, while it is the only heaven the unbelievers will ever experience.

    iv) Storms come to also those who are in God's will. It is deception to think that if you are in God's will, no storms will come.

d) **Satan**

As we previously studied in Chapter Four, Satan is often the one responsible for the evil we see in the world today.

"The thief cometh not, but for to steal, and to kill, and to destroy: I am come that they might have life, and that they might have it more abundantly." (John 10:10). Satan is one of the main reasons we experience stealing, killing, and destroying.

    i) Look no further, this verse among many others **clearly spells out who kills, steals, and destroys**.

       • Satan is the thief, killer, and destroyer NOT God. The devil is another reason that bad things happen.

    ii) Every tragedy, sickness, disease, death and so forth can be categorized into these three things–**stealing, killing, and destruction**.

- If there is any stealing, killing, and destruction it is Satan (Devil) who is behind it NOT God.

"How art thou fallen from heaven, O Lucifer, son of the morning! How art thou cut down to the ground, which didst weaken the nations! For thou hast said in thine heart, I will ascend into heaven, I will exalt my throne above the stars of God: I will sit also upon the mount of the congregation, in the sides of the north: I will ascend above the heights of the clouds; I will be like the most High. Yet thou shalt be brought down to hell, to the sides of the pit. They that see thee shall narrowly look upon thee, and consider thee, saying, Is this the man that made the earth to tremble, that did shake kingdoms; That made the world as a wilderness, and destroyed the cities thereof; that opened not the house of his prisoners?"

—Isaiah 14:12-17

These verses talk about Lucifer who is well known today as Satan. These verses clearly show that Satan or Lucifer is the one responsible for the evil and tragedy happening in the world.

It says he:

- Made the world a wilderness
- Destroyed cities
- Imprisoned people (Spiritually and physically)

This flies in the face of those who say God is the one who causes evil and tragedy. These verses clearly say that it is Lucifer (Satan) NOT God.

e) **Individual sins**

"Afterward Jesus findeth him in the temple, and said unto him, Behold, thou art made whole: sin no more, lest a worse thing come unto thee."

—John 5:14

i) This response from Jesus clearly indicates that living in sin or sinful lifestyle could cause bad things to come upon us.

- If we change the way we are living, we stop certain things from happening.
- If we continue to live in sin anyhow, we open a door (Romans 6:16 and James 4:7) to the devil who comes in to steal, kill and destroy (John 10:10).

ii) Also, it shows that what this man was going through was **self-inflicted**.

- Living in sin opened a door to this man's life and as a result, he was diseased for 38 years.
- It is clear enough that God had nothing to do with this man's disease, nonetheless, He came to his rescue and made him whole.

f) **Nature (creation) groaning**

"Because the creature itself also shall be delivered from the bondage of corruption into the glorious liberty of the children of God. For we know that the whole creation groaneth and travaileth in pain together until now. And not only they, but ourselves also, which have the firstfruits of the Spirit, even we ourselves groan within ourselves, waiting for the adoption, to wit, the redemption of our body."

–Romans 8:21-22

i) One of the main reasons we see the mess of storms, earthquakes, and hurricanes, is **because the earth is groaning in birth pains**.

- The corruption of sin that happened in the garden affected every bit of creation including the earth.

ii) The word *"GROANETH"* used in this verse is translated from a Greek word that means *"to moan jointly, that is, (figuratively) experience a common calamity."* (Strong's Concordance).

- So, this is saying that the earth experienced a common calamity, and therefore, is moaning.

- This moaning (groaning) has caused lots of tragedies that people blame on God. This will continue until the full redemption of the Children of God.

g) **Evil people**

"Know ye not, that to whom ye yield yourselves servants to obey, his servants ye are to whom ye obey; whether of sin unto death, or of obedience unto righteousness?"

–Romans 6:16

i) Satan works through people. There are some evil people out there.

- When someone does evil to you, do not blame God. It's the person that has done it–not God.

- Don't get mad at God. We live in a world where people yield themselves to be vessels and instruments of Satan.

- This is another channel through which bad things happen to us. If people make themselves instruments for Satan, they will cause bad things to happen. Death, disease, sickness, suffering, and many things happen because of people who are in unity with the devil.

ii) *"From whence come wars and fightings among you? Come they not hence, even of your lusts that war in your members?"* –James 4:1.

- People's lust is one of the causes of bad things and evils we encounter.

h) **Ignorance of the Word**

"My people are destroyed for lack of knowledge: because thou hast rejected knowledge, I will also reject thee, that thou shalt be no priest to me: seeing

thou hast forgotten the law of thy God, I will also forget thy children."

–Hosea 4:6

i) There is a degree of responsibility that believers or the church have to take for their passiveness.

ii) Ignorance of the Word of God only allows the works of the Enemy to prevail unchecked and unchallenged. Ignorance of the Word has led to wrong believing, therefore no results.

iii) *"Jesus answered and said unto them, Ye do err, not knowing the scriptures, nor the power of God."* –Matthew 22:29

i) Not using our God-given authority

"Behold, I give unto you power to tread on serpents and scorpions, and over all the power of the enemy: and nothing shall by any means hurt you."

–Luke 10:19

i) God has given the believers and the body of Christ **power and authority** over the works of the devil such as sickness, poverty, death and destruction, but many do not know they have it nor do they use it.

ii) He has also given us the name of Jesus which is the name above all names (John 14:13; Philippians 2:9-11). He has given us the faith of Jesus and the commission to do "greater works" (John 14:12).

iii) *"Submit yourselves therefore to God. Resist the devil, and he will flee from you."* –James 4:7

j) Consequences for our actions

"For he that soweth to his flesh shall of the flesh reap corruption; but he that soweth to the Spirit shall of the Spirit reap life everlasting."

–Galatians 6:8

i) This verse makes it clear that of the flesh we reap corruption—not of God.

ii) Those who blame God have missed what this verse teaches.

k) Death comes by sin

"For the wages of sin is death; but the gift of God is eternal life through Jesus Christ our Lord."

—Romans 6:23

*"Wherefore, as by one man sin entered into the world, and **death by sin**; and so death passed upon all men, for that all have sinned."*

—Romans 5:12

i) This verse says that death **comes by sin, not by God**. Another way to say this is that the wages which sin pays is death. This does not say that God pays wages of death—no, it is sin.

Notice that God is not on that list above as to why bad things happen. He should NOT be. He is not the One behind all the misery, sickness, plunder, sin, killing, destroying, and stealing. Let me end with these lyrics by *Annie J. Flint*:

"He giveth more grace when the burdens grow greater, He sendeth more strength when the labors increase; To added afflictions He addeth His mercy, To multiplied trials, His multiplied peace.

When we have exhausted our store of endurance, When our strength has failed ere the day is half done, When we reach the end of our hoarded resources, Our Father's full giving is only begun.

Fear not that thy need shall exceed His provision, Our God ever yearns His resources to share; Lean hard on the arm everlasting, availing; The Father both thee and thy load will upbear.

His love has no limits, His grace has no measure, His power no boundary known unto men; For out of His infinite riches in Jesus He giveth, and giveth, and giveth again."

Chapter Nineteen

How Should a Christian Vote? Republican, Democrat, or Independent?

Many people are party bound. They always vote along party lines even if their party violates their biblical Christian values and beliefs. How sad! I have come to understand that although people make this a party thing: Republican versus Democrat, the very truth is this is a moral versus immoral fight, right versus wrong, godly versus ungodly (Proverbs 29:27), not necessarily Republican versus Democrat. To only look at the party name is to miss the very point of what is going on behind the scenes.

We need to find out the platform of the party or individual we want to vote for and make sure it does not violate biblical godly principles such as marriage (between a man and a woman), pro-life (against abortion), and encourages employment and hard work and not laziness and government dependency (2 Thessalonians 3:10), strong families, limited government, honesty and integrity, compassion, personal responsibility, freedom, and rule of law. Christians should not go into hiding or refuse to get involved in the democratic process of voting. This way, we get the moral majority to rule which is good for both the godly and the ungodly. I believe that the vast majority of religious, godly, and moral people are conservatives, and the opposite is true as pertains to the liberals. If we want godliness and morality to prevail, we the conservatives, the godly and moral people, have to come out of our closets. We have nothing to fear and hide. We are on the right side of things. If the liberals and ungodly like the pro-choice and LGBT have come out of their closets, should we stay in ours? Salt has to leave its shaker to be of any good. We must learn to make God's Word our primary voting guide. The Bible says, "Thy word is a lamp unto my feet, and a light unto my path." (Psalm 119:105).

When we vote for the ungodly, we should not blame God for the aftermath of our decisions. Proverbs 29:16 says, "When the wicked are multiplied, transgression increaseth: but the righteous shall see their fall." **We need to vote for a candidate who upholds Christian principles; whose ability to lead well has already been demonstrated; who is able to lead our country with justice and is God-fearing**. True, all candidates may not be godly, but we have to look for the one who represents our godly and biblical values more than the others. Even among two ungodly people, we can find one whose principles best align with God's. We should not stand by or sit out and let evil and ungodliness prevail only because we do not like a certain candidate. Additionally, we should also support the candidate that can win. It would be a waste to support any candidate that can't win because he or she will be spoiling the vote and the support that a potential candidate would need to win.

For example, during the 2016 presidential elections, Christians were left with a choice of three candidates: Donald J. Trump (R), Hillary Clinton (D), and independent candidate Jill Stein. Stein had no chance of winning. Any vote for her was a waste. It makes no sense to vote for the godliest person that cannot win. That is a wasted vote.

On the other hand, we had two candidates left, of which they were both not very godly candidates, but looking at the principles that they ran on, it was more than clear who was godlier than the other. Donald Trump supported marriage (man and woman), was against abortion, was in support of sending people to work and getting them off the government dependency. He was for a limited government, for putting America first not last, and finally, he vocally expressed his belief in the Bible as God's Holy Word. All of this was the antithesis of what Hilary Clinton represented and stood for.

"Righteousness exalteth a nation: but sin is a reproach to any people."

–Proverbs 14:34

We must be very cautious about how we vote, for it will affect us whether we believe it or not. Our voting should be an attempt to exalt righteousness or the righteous, not the ungodly and ungodliness. I always believe in voting for the Bible and for godliness. I don't vote for personality, influence, appearance, or charisma. Seldom are you going to find a very godly politician; therefore, it is wisest to vote for the godliest person available that can win. There is no perfect man and if that is the standard you are looking for; you will never find any. We are to vote for those policies and godly principles that advance or uphold the kingdom of God. We should not be voting for baby killers. Abortion is ungodly. God is pro-life, not pro-choice. He is pro traditional marriage between a man and a woman, not same sex marriage, not bestiality, nor incest. God is pro hard work, not government dependency.

> *"The only thing necessary for the triumph of evil is that good men should do nothing."*
>
> –Edmund Burke

One of the major reasons why ungodliness is prevailing and growing rampantly is because the church and the Christians have been in hiding. They have not gotten involved in this process of voting and turning things around. They have been deceived into only praying and sitting on their hands with zero action and participation. The truth is that we have a privilege, responsibility, and a right to get involved and turn things around for the kingdom of God. We must get involved or else things will never change. Christians should be involved in all the seven mountains of influence, including **Religion & Faith; Family; Education; Government (Politics) & Law; Media, News & Commentary; Arts & Entertainment**; and **Business & Economics**. We need born-again Christians in all these seven mountains of influence of society, not just the Religion & Faith mountain, but far beyond that including the political arena. Furthermore, here in the United States, we need to refute the lie of **"separation of church and state."** I'm sure that you have heard this phrase. It is probably the best-known phrase in America, yet it is the least understood. Many people, especially those that hate Christianity, have used this phrase to build a wall of separation between one's personal faith and any public display of that faith.

The First Amendment of the U.S. Constitution clearly states and says, "Congress shall make no law respecting an establishment of religion or prohibiting the free exercise thereof; or abridging the freedom of speech, or of the press; or the right of the people peaceably to assemble, and to petition the Government for a redress of grievances."

The famous phrase of separation of church and state is nowhere in that first amendment of the US Constitution nor the Declaration of Independence. This makes it clear that we can exercise our faith, wherever we are, including public schools, governmental venues, and the public square freely. This phrase first appeared in a letter written by Thomas Jefferson to the Danbury Baptist Association of Connecticut in 1801. Many people present it as if it were a part of the Constitution. There is nothing like "separation of church and state" in the Constitution. It is made up and designed to silence the freedom of religion and faith.

In an article written by Mr. David Barton (Wallbuilders.com) on *How to Respond to "Separation of Church and State,"* he says,

"Thomas Jefferson had worked very hard to separate the Anglican Church from the government in his home state of Virginia so that all other denominations could practice their faith without government penalty or persecution. Jefferson contributed to ending government-run religion in his state, so when he became president of the United States, the Baptists and those from other denominations were his strong supporters because he had fought for their freedom of religion–for their right to be free from state control in matters of faith.

The Danbury Baptists wrote Thomas Jefferson expressing their concern that the government might try to regulate their religious expression. In response, Jefferson wrote his now famous letter, using the phrase 'Separation of Church and State' to reassure the Danbury Baptists that the First Amendment prohibited the government from trying to control religious expression. In short, the First Amendment was intended to keep government out of regulating religion, but it did not keep religion out of government or the public square."

We should not be intimidated by the IRS to keep silent and not get involved in the political and government arenas because of fear that they will take away our tax exemption status. Big deal, they can take it back. I would rather lose my tax exemption than let people's lives be destroyed by ungodliness and go to hell only because I will not speak up in fear of the government revoking my tax exemption. Matter of fact, the Lord Jesus and the Apostle Paul preached the Gospel into the world without tax exemption and made a great impact. So can we.

> *"When the righteous are in authority, the people rejoice: but when the wicked beareth rule, the people mourn."*
>
> —Proverbs 29:2

This verse clearly says that if we get the ungodly into authority, we should forget rejoicing. Rejoicing is a byproduct of the godly being in authority. On the other hand, when the wicked and ungodly rule, people mourn and suffer as a result.

> *"You can be a believer and a liberal, but you can't be a disciple and a liberal."*
>
> — Andrew Wommack.

As stated previously, there is a difference between a disciple and a convert. Disciples do not vote for people, they vote for the Bible (biblical values and principles), while the convert votes for people, emotion, charisma, looks, education, skin color, etc. God's Word has a lot to say about the issues we face today in all societies, but for us to have an impact on our societies, we must graduate to being disciples not just converts. Through God's Word, we must develop a biblical worldview, approach, and perspective on all things and speak up. We ought to be the light of the world and the salt of the earth, and one of the best ways to be effective in that is to study and continue in God's Word. We should develop a discipleship mentality.

Conservative vs. Liberal Beliefs

We all want the same things in life. We want freedom; we want the chance for prosperity; we want as few people suffering as possible; we want healthy children; we want to have crime-free streets. The argument is how to achieve them…

Liberals believe in government action to achieve equal opportunity and equality for all. It is the duty of the government to alleviate social ills and to protect civil liberties and individual and human rights. They believe the role of the government should be to guarantee that no one is in need. Liberal policies generally emphasize the need for the government to solve problems.

Conservatives believe in personal responsibility, limited government, free markets, individual liberty, traditional American values, and a strong national defense. They believe the role of government should be to provide people the freedom necessary to pursue their own goals. Conservative policies generally emphasize empowerment of the individual to solve problems.

NOTE: The terms "left" and "right" define opposite ends of the political spectrum. In the United States, liberals are referred to as the left or left-wing and conservatives are referred to as the right or right-wing. On the U.S. political map, blue represents the Democratic Party (which generally upholds liberal principles) and red represents the Republican Party (which generally upholds conservative principles)."

I have organized and put these issues in a table for easy access, reference, and study. After studying this detailed table explaining all the facts on these subjects or issues, you should be able to determine which side you belong to. However, it is evident that the side that best reflects the beliefs, principles, and values of the Bible is the conservative side.

"Not being heard is no reason for silence." –Victor Hugo

"Silence in the face of evil is evil itself. God will not hold us guiltless. Not to speak is to speak. Not to act is to act."–Dietrich Bonhoeffer (When opposing Hitler during WWII.)

Issues or Subject	Conservative	Liberal
Abortion	• Human life begins at conception. • Abortion is the murder of a human being. • An unborn baby, as a living human being, has separate rights from those of the mother. • Oppose taxpayer-funded abortion. • Taxpayer dollars should not be used for the government to provide abortions and fund actions that taxpayers do not approve of. Support legislation to prohibit partial birth abortions, called the "Partial Birth Abortion* Ban" (*Partial Birth Abortion: the killing of an unborn baby of at least 20 weeks by pulling it out of the birth canal with forceps, but leaving the head inside. An incision is made in the back of the baby's neck and the brain tissue is suctioned out. The head is then removed from the uterus.) • Why would an adult make adult decisions and actions and not expect adult responsibilities, repercussions, and consequences? • "I've noticed that everyone who is for abortion is already born" –Ronald Reagan	• A woman has the right to decide what happens with her body. • A fetus is not a human life, so it does not have separate individual rights. • The government should provide taxpayer funded abortions for women who cannot afford them. • The decision to have an abortion is a personal choice of a woman regarding her own body and the government must protect this right. • Women have the right to affordable, safe and legal abortions, including partial birth abortion.

Affirmative Action	• Individuals should be admitted to schools and hired for jobs based on their ability. • It is unfair to use race as a factor in the selection process. • **Reverse-discrimination** is not a solution for racism. • Some individuals in society are racist, but American society as a whole is not. • Preferential treatment of certain races through affirmative action is wrong.	• Due to prevalent racism in the past, minorities were deprived of the same education and employment opportunities as whites. • The government must work to make up for that. America is still a racist society; therefore, a federal affirmative action law is necessary. Due to unequal opportunity, minorities still lag behind whites in all statistical measurements of success.
Death Penalty	• **The death penalty is a punishment that fits the crime of murder; it is neither "cruel" nor "unusual". Executing a murderer is the appropriate punishment for taking an innocent life.** • It is a biblical principle and a deterrent to violent crimes such as murder so that others do not emulate the act for their own fame and glory.	• **The death penalty should be abolished.** • It is inhumane and is "cruel and unusual" punishment. Imprisonment is the appropriate punishment for murder. • Every execution risks killing an innocent person.
Economy	• The free market system, competitive capitalism, and private enterprise create the greatest opportunity and the highest standard of living for all. • Free markets produce more economic growth, more jobs, and higher standards of living than those systems burdened by excessive government regulation.	• A market system in which government regulates the economy is best. • Government must protect citizens from the greed of big business. Unlike the private sector, the government is motivated by public interest. • Government regulation in all areas of the economy is needed to level the playing field.

Education – vouchers & charter schools	• **School vouchers create competition and therefore encourage schools to improve performance.** • Vouchers will give all parents the right to choose good schools for their children, not just those who can afford private schools.	• **Public schools are the best way to educate students.** • **Vouchers take money away from public schools.** • Government should focus additional funds on existing public schools, raising teacher salaries and reducing class size.
Embryonic Stem Cell Research	• Support the use of _adult and umbilical cord stem cells only_ **for research**. • It is morally and ethically wrong for the government to fund _embryonic stem cell research_. • Human life begins at conception. • The extraction of stem cells from an embryo requires its destruction. In other words, it requires that a human life be killed. • _Adult stem cells_ have already been used to treat spinal cord injuries, Leukemia, and even Parkinson's disease. _Adult stem cells_ are derived from umbilical cords, placentas, amniotic fluid, various tissues and organ systems like skin and the liver, and even fat obtained from liposuction. _Embryonic stem cells_ have not been successfully used to help cure disease.	• Support the use of **embryonic stem cells for research**. • It is necessary (and ethical) for the government to fund embryonic stem cell research, which will assist scientists in finding treatments and cures for diseases. • **An embryo is not a human.** • The tiny blastocyst (embryos used in embryonic stem cell research) has no human features. • Experimenting on embryos/embryonic stem cells is not murder. • _Embryonic stem cells_ have the potential to cure chronic and degenerative diseases which current medicine has been unable to effectively treat. _Embryonic stem cells_ have been shown to be effective in treating heart damage in mice.

Energy	**Oil, gas, and coal are all good sources of energy and are abundant in the U.S.** Oil drilling should be increased both on land and at sea. Increased domestic production creates lower prices and less dependence on other countries for oil. Support increased production of nuclear energy. Wind and solar sources will never provide plentiful, affordable sources of power. Support private ownership of gas and electric industries.	• **Oil is a depleting resource. Other sources of energy must be explored.** • The government must produce a national plan for all energy resources and subsidize (partially pay for) alternative energy research and production. • Support increased exploration of alternative energy sources such as wind and solar power. • Support government control of gas and electric industries.
Euthanasia & Physician-assisted suicide	• **Neither euthanasia nor physician-assisted suicide should be legalized.** • **It is immoral and unethical to deliberately end the life of a terminally ill person** (euthanasia) or enable another person to end their own life (assisted suicide). • The goal should be compassionate care and easing the suffering of terminally ill people. • **Legalizing euthanasia could lead to doctor-assisted suicides of non-critical patients.** • **If euthanasia were legalized, insurance companies could pressure doctors to withhold life-saving treatment for dying patients.**	• **Euthanasia should be legalized.** • **A person has a right to die with dignity, by his own choice.** • **A terminally ill person should have the right to choose to end pain and suffering.** • **It is wrong for the government to take away the means for a terminally ill person to hasten his death.** • It is wrong to force a person to go through so much pain and suffering. Legalizing euthanasia would not lead to doctor-assisted suicides of non-critical patients. Permitting euthanasia would reduce health care

	• Many religions prohibit suicide and euthanasia. These practices devalue human life.	costs, which would then make funds available for those who could truly benefit from medical care.
Global Warming/ Climate Change	• Change in global temperature is natural over long periods of time. • Science has not shown that humans can affect permanent change to the earth's temperature. • Proposed laws to reduce carbon emissions will do nothing to help the environment and will cause significant price increases for all. Many reputable scientists support this theory.	• Global warming is caused by an increased production of carbon dioxide through the burning of fossil fuels (coal, oil, and natural gas). The U.S. is a major contributor to global warming because it produces 25% of the world's carbon dioxide. Proposed laws to reduce carbon emissions in the U.S. are urgently needed and should be enacted immediately to save the planet. Many reputable scientists support this theory.
Gun Control	• The Second Amendment gives citizens the right to keep and bear arms. Individuals have the right to defend themselves. • There are too many gun control laws–additional laws will not lower gun crime rates. What is needed is enforcement of current laws. • Gun control laws do not prevent criminals from obtaining guns. More guns in the hands of law-abiding citizens mean less crime. • *Full text of the Second Amendment to the U.S. Constitution: "A well regulated Militia, being necessary*	• The Second Amendment does not give citizens the right to keep and bear arms, but only allows for the state to keep a militia (National Guard). • Individuals do not need guns for protection; it is the role of local and federal government to protect the people through law enforcement agencies and the military. • Additional gun control laws are necessary to stop gun violence and limit the ability of criminals to obtain guns. More guns means more violence.

	to the security of a free State, the right of the people to keep and bear Arms, shall not be infringed."	
Healthcare	• **Support competitive, free market health care system. All Americans have access to health care.** The debate is about who should pay for it. • **Free and low-cost government-run programs (socialized medicine) result in higher costs and everyone receiving the same poor-quality health care.** • **Health care should remain privatized.** • The problem of uninsured individuals should be addressed and solved within the free market healthcare system–the government should not control healthcare.	• **Support free or low-cost government-controlled health care.** • **There are millions of Americans who can't afford health care and are deprived of this basic right.** • Every American has a right to affordable health care. • The government should provide equal health care benefits for all, regardless of their ability to pay.
Homeland Security	• Airport security – Choosing passengers randomly for extra security searches is not effective. • Rather, profiling and intelligence data should be used to single out passengers for extra screening. • Those who do not meet the criteria for suspicion should not be subjected to intense screening.	• Airport security – Passenger profiling is wrong, period. • Selection of passengers for extra security screening should be random. • Using other criteria (such as ethnicity) is discriminatory and offensive to Arabs and Muslims, who are generally innocent and law-abiding. Terrorists don't fit a profile.

	• The terrorists currently posing a threat to the U.S. are primarily Islamic/Muslim men between the ages of 18 and 38. • Our resources should be focused on this group. • Profiling is good logical police work. *"If people are offended (by profiling), that's unfortunate, but I don't think we can afford to take the risk that terrorism brings to us. They've wasted masses of resources on far too many people doing things that really don't have a big payoff in terms of security."* –Northwestern University Aviation Expert, A. Gellman.	• "…Arabs, Muslims and South Asians are no more likely than whites to be terrorists." (American Civil Liberties Union ACLU) • Asked on 60 Minutes if a 70-year-old white woman from Vero Beach should receive the same level of scrutiny as a Muslim from Jersey City, President Obama's Transportation Secretary Norman Mineta said, "Basically, I would hope so."
Immigration	• **Support legal immigration only.** • **Oppose amnesty for those who enter the U.S. illegally (illegal immigrants).** • **Those who break the law by entering the U.S. illegally do not have the same rights as those who obey the law and enter legally.** • **The borders should be secured before addressing the problem of the illegal immigrants currently in the country.** • **The Federal Government should secure the borders and enforce current immigration law.**	• **Support legal immigration and more.** • **Support amnesty for those who enter the U.S. illegally (undocumented immigrants).**

Private Property	• Respect ownership and private property rights. • Eminent domain (seizure of private property by the government–with compensation to the owner) in most cases is wrong. Eminent domain should not be used for private development.	• Government has the right to use eminent domain (seizure of private property by the government with compensation to the owner) to accomplish a public end.
Religion & Government	• The phrase *"separation of church and state"* is not in the Constitution. • The First Amendment to the Constitution states *"Congress shall make no law respecting an establishment of religion, or prohibiting the free exercise thereof..."* • This prevents the government from establishing a national church/denomination. However, it does not prohibit God from being acknowledged in schools and government buildings. Symbols of Christian heritage should not be removed from public and government spaces (e.g. the Ten Commandments should continue to be displayed in Federal buildings). Government should not interfere with religion and religious freedom.	• Support the separation of church and state. The Bill of Rights implies a separation of church and state. • **Religious expression has no place in government.** • The two should be completely separate. Government should not support religious expression in any way. All reference to God in public and government spaces should be removed (e.g. the Ten Commandments should not be displayed in Federal buildings). Religious expression has no place in government.

Same-sex Marriage	• Marriage is the union of one man and one woman. • Oppose same-sex marriage. • Support Defense of Marriage Act (DOMA), passed in 1996, which affirms the right of states not to recognize same-sex marriages licensed in other states. • Requiring citizens to sanction same-sex relationships violates moral and religious beliefs of millions of Christians, Jews, Muslims, and others, who believe marriage is the union of one man and one woman.	• Marriage is the union of people who love each other. • It should be legal for gay, lesbian, bisexual and transgender individuals, to ensure equal rights for all. Support same-sex marriage. • Opposed to the creation of a constitutional amendment establishing marriage as the union of one man and one woman. • All individuals, regardless of their sexual orientation, have **the right to marry**. Prohibiting same-sex citizens from marrying denies them their civil rights. [Opinions vary on whether this issue is equal to civil rights for African Americans.]
Social Security	• **The Social Security system is in serious financial trouble.** • Major changes to the current system are urgently needed. In its current state, the Social Security system is not financially sustainable. It will collapse if nothing is done to address the problems. Many will suffer as a result. • **Social Security must be made more efficient through privatization and/or allowing individuals to manage their own savings.**	• The Social Security system should be protected at all costs. Reduction in future benefits is not a reasonable option. [Opinions vary on the extent of the current system's financial stability.] • Social Security provides a safety net for the nation's poor and needy. • **Changing the system would cause a reduction in benefits and many people would suffer as a result.**

Taxes	• **Lower taxes and a smaller government with limited power will improve the standard of living for all.** • **Support lower taxes and a smaller government.** • **Lower taxes create more incentive for people to work, save, invest, and engage in entrepreneurial endeavors.** • **Money is best spent by those who earn it, not the government. Government programs encourage people to become dependent and lazy, rather than encouraging work and independence.**	• **Higher taxes (primarily for the wealthy) and a larger government are necessary to address inequity/injustice in society (government should help the poor and needy using tax dollars from the rich).** • **Support a large government to provide for the needs of the people and create equality.** • Taxes enable the government to create jobs and provide welfare programs for those in need. Government programs are a caring way to provide for the poor and needy in society.
United Nations (UN)	• The UN has repeatedly failed in its essential mission to promote world peace and human rights. The wars, genocide and human rights abuses taking place in many Human Rights Council member states (and the UN's failure to stop them) prove this point. • History shows that the United States, not the UN, is the global force for spreading freedom, prosperity, tolerance and peace. • **The U.S. should never subvert its national interests to those of the UN.** • **The U.S. should never place troops under UN control.**	• The UN promotes peace and human rights. The United States has a moral and a legal obligation to support the United Nations (UN). • **The U.S. should not act as a sovereign nation, but as one member of a world community.** • The U.S. should submit its national interests to the greater good of the global community (as defined by the UN). The U.S. should defer to the UN in military/peacekeeping matters. • The United Nations Charter gives the United Nations Security Council the power and responsibility to take

	• U.S. military should always wear the U.S. military uniform, not that of UN peacekeepers. [Opinions vary on whether the U.S. should withdraw from the UN.]	collective action to maintain international peace and security. • **U.S. troops should submit to UN command.**
War On Terror/ Terrorism	• **Terrorism poses one of the greatest threats to the U.S.** • The world toward which the militant Islamists strive cannot peacefully co-exist with the Western world. • In the last decade, militant Islamists have repeatedly attacked Americans and American interests here and abroad. • **Terrorists must be stopped and destroyed.** • The use of intelligence-gathering and military force are the best ways to defeat terrorism around the world. • Captured terrorists should be treated as enemy combatants and tried in military courts.	• **Global warming**, not terrorism, poses the greatest threat to the U.S., according to Democrats in Congress. • Terrorism is a result of arrogant U.S. foreign policy. • **Good diplomacy is the best way to deal with terrorism.** • Relying on military force to defeat terrorism creates hatred that leads to more terrorism. • Captured terrorists should be handled by law enforcement and tried in civilian courts.
Welfare	• **Oppose long-term welfare.** • Opportunities should be provided to make it possible for those in need to become self-reliant. • **It is far more compassionate and effective to encourage people to become**	• **Support welfare, including long-term welfare.** • Welfare is a safety net which provides for the needs of the poor. • Welfare is necessary to bring fairness to American economic life. It is a device for protecting the poor.

	self-reliant, rather than allowing them to remain dependent on the government for provisions.	

I have edited this table and made some changes to it, but the overall piece was **Compiled by the Editors at StudentNewsDaily.com Copyright 2005 (revised 2010)**.

Lastly, I want to add the subject of **infanticide**, which is the latest publicly promoted evil of our society at the time in my writing this book. First, let me boldly say, I have discovered that one of the main reasons that people support or legislate in favor of abortion and infanticide is so that they can profit from the selling of the body parts of these babies. Employees of a shameful renowned organization– *Planned Parenthood*, a chief in slaughtering babies in the womb and after the womb were later exposed on video for selling the body parts harvested in abortion. What a shame! This is evil and ungodly.

Back to infanticide, Infanticide is the crime of killing an infant or a child within a year of birth especially one who has survived the act of abortion.

Recently in February 2019, Senator Ben Sasse of Nebraska proposed a simple bill in the United States Senate. It's called the Born-Alive Abortion Survivors Protection Act (S. 311). It had one objective, and that was **to force lawmakers to go on the record about whether they support or oppose infanticide**.

The summary of the bill by Ben Sasse read along these lines, "If an abortion results in the live birth of an infant, the infant is a legal person for all purposes under the laws of the United States," and the Constitution, "and entitled to all the protections of such laws."

What were the results? The bill failed because it was opposed. The final vote was 53 to 44. They needed 60 votes for the bill to pass. A bunch of Democrats and among them several Democrat candidates for the Democratic presidential nomination in 2020 (Sens. Cory Booker (N.J.), Sherrod Brown (Ohio), Kirsten Gillibrand (N.Y.), Kamala Harris (Calif.), Amy Klobuchar (Minn.), Jeff Merkley (Ore.) and Elizabeth Warren (Mass.)–plus independent Sen. Bernie Sanders (Vt.)–voted against the Born-Alive Abortion Survivors Protection Act.

All democrats apart from three (Democratic Sens. Bob Casey (Pa.), Doug Jones (Ala.) and Joe Manchin (W.Va.) voted in favor of this bill. All the rest of the democrats voted to block (against) the bill. In other words, they voted for infanticide.

Three Republicans did not vote. Senators Kevin Cramer of North Dakota, Lisa Murkowski of Alaska, Tim Scott of South Carolina. However, Cramer and Scott missed the vote due to flight delays. They had intentions to vote for it. They just didn't get there. So, it would have been 55-42. You can clearly see which side the godly side based on this issue of Infanticide. Who in the world would be in favor of killing a born child that has survived abortion, not to mention a child in the womb? The Democrats in the U.S. Congress, that's who. It is a shame that people would support such an ungodly position to kill born-alive abortion survivors. Who knows what is next? These Democrat jokers could be voting for killing your child or grandchild next, if not your grandma. If Jesus were present in the US Senate, which side would He vote with? **Yes, the Republican side–He would have voted in favor of the bill–NOT to kill the born-alive abortion survivors** who the democrats voted to kill.

We have to speak up, yet not just in the US, but also around the World. Evil is evil no matter where it is. All the godly folks ought to oppose and speak up against such.

"Not being heard is no reason for silence." –Victor Hugo

"Silence in the face of evil is evil itself. God will not hold us guiltless. Not to speak is to speak. Not to act is to act." – Dietrich Bonhoeffer (When opposing Hitler during WWII.)

I want to leave you with this powerful quote from President Ronald Reagan: *"In the Bible's pages lie the answers to all problems that mankind has ever known. I hope Americans will read and study the bible."*

Conclusion

I know I have shared quite a bit and I do believe that the Lord has spoken to you in at least one area of your life. We all have questions and if we desire to see them answered and also be able to help those that struggle, the Lord will surely answer them.

By the same token, we have to remember that we know in part (1 Corinthians 13:9). As much as I desire to answer all questions people encounter, we need to learn to go to God and His Word for these things to be answered. I'm only a form of help, we need to build our lives and draw answers through our relationship with Him. As we grow in our relationship with God, we will come to a place where we are fully satisfied and have all our questions answered.

Receive Jesus As Your Savior

Deciding to receive Jesus Christ as your Lord and Savior is the most important decision you'll ever make! Nothing comes close to this decision; not your career and not even your spouse. It will change your life now and your eternal destiny. There is no decision that could be made that is like it. It would be very sad for me to teach you that Jesus was and is God and not give you an opportunity to repent and to receive Him into your heart as your God and Savior. Will you accept Him as God and not just another good man like some believe and say?

God has promised, *"If thou shalt confess with thy mouth the Lord Jesus, and shalt believe in thine heart that God hath raised him from the dead, thou shalt be saved. For with the heart man believeth unto righteousness; and with the mouth confession is made unto salvation.... For whosoever shall call upon the name of the Lord shall be saved."* (Romans 10:9-10, 13).

By His grace, God has already done everything on His part to provide for your salvation. Your part is simply to believe and receive. It is the easiest decision. This is a heart decision, not a head decision. Now is the acceptable time, today is the day of salvation (2 Corinthians 6:2). Why wait?

Pray this prayer and mean it sincerely from your heart:

Lord Jesus,
I confess that You are my Lord and Savior. I believe in my heart that God raised You from the dead. By faith in Your Word, I receive salvation, now. Thank You for saving me!

The very moment you commit your life to Jesus Christ, the truth of His Word instantly comes to pass in your spirit. Now that you're born again, you are brand new on the inside. God has created in you a new spirit and a new heart.

Receive the Baptism of the Holy Spirit

Living a Christian life is not just a difficult thing to do but an impossible thing. You need help. So, because it is impossible to live a victorious, Christian life without the baptism of the Holy Spirit, the Lord wants to give you the supernatural power you need to live this new life. We receive power when we receive the baptism of the Holy Spirit (Acts 1:8).

It's as simple as asking and receiving. When we ask for the Holy Spirit, the Lord will give Him to us (Luke 11:10, 13).

All you have to do is ask, believe, and receive! Pray:

Father, I recognize my need for Your power to live this new life. Please fill me with Your Holy Spirit. By faith, I receive Him right now! Thank You for baptizing me. Holy Spirit, You are welcome in my life.

Congratulations! Now you're filled with God's supernatural power. Some syllables from a language you don't recognize will rise up from your heart to your mouth (See 1 Corinthians 14:14). Go ahead and speak those syllables. As you speak them out loud by faith, you're releasing God's power from within and building yourself up in the Spirit (See 1 Corinthians 14:4). You can do this whenever and wherever you like.

It doesn't really matter whether you felt anything or not when you prayed to receive the Lord and His Spirit. If you believed in your heart that you received, then God's Word promises that you received. *"Therefore, I say unto you, What things soever ye desire, when ye pray, believe that ye receive them, and ye shall have them"* (Mark 11:24). God always honors His Word—believe it!

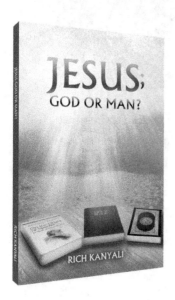

Jesus; God or Man?

by Rich Kanyali

Paperback

ISBN: 978-1513627113

eBook is also available

In this book, Rich takes you on a journey to discover a certain truth that distinguishes Christianity from any other religion, faith, or belief system. Have you ever given a single thought as to whether Jesus was God or man?

To some, Jesus was a good man. To some, He was a great historical figure. To some, He was god (not divine). To some, He was a god among many other gods. To some, an angel (Michael the Archangel). To some, a prophet, but to others, He was and is God. So, which is which? What category do you fall into? Was Jesus God or man? Within the pages of this book, you will find powerful biblical proof and sound reasoning to who Jesus truly was and is. The evidence is within the pages of this book. The truth is unveiled leaving no stone unturned. Reading this book will shed light unto your understanding and give you a greater revelation of this truth.

Good Health and Long life: Another Perspective

by Rich Kanyali

Paperback

ISBN: 978-1642044201

In Good Health & Long Life–Another Perspective, Rich writes to give a different perspective on health and long life. Many times, the only focus on health is what we do physically such as what we eat, how we exercise and so forth. However, there is a very much untapped side of health which is even more important than even the physical. In this book, Rich explores this side and how we can enhance our health and achieve long life.

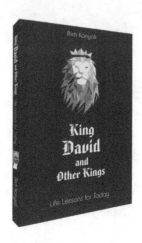

King David and Other Kings:
Life Lessons for Today

by Rich Kanyali

Paperback

ISBN: 978-1-64370-623-8

eBook is also available

Life is a life of lessons. We can learn from those that went before us and those that are still with us. Although the life of King David was more like a roller coaster, it's one of the most detailed lives we have in the Holy Scriptures. We see the good and the ugly of his life. He made some wrong decisions and he made some great ones too. Nonetheless, the Word of God says that he was a "Man after God's own heart." One thing Rich does not recommend is always learning by your own experience. Sometimes the best way is to learn is from the experience of another. We can learn at David's expense (1 Corinthians 10:1-12).

In this book, *King David and Other Kings*, Rich draws out those lessons we can learn from the life of David before and after he was King, and how to avoid the same pitfalls that he fell into. He goes a little further and throws in a bonus of five other kings such as Jehu, Saul, Jehoshaphat, Manasseh, and Josiah as comparisons and contrasts to King David. You will love what you read, and you will find the application of these truths in your life transformational and impactful as Rich has.

Where is Your Prosperity: Countering a Third World Mentality and Learning to Trust God Wherever You Are

by Rich Kanyali

Paperback

ISBN: 978-1-646060-085-6

None of us chooses where we are born and while some places are more prosperous than others, how do people in some of these less developed or underdeveloped countries prosper? Do they have to relocate to another country, or can they prosper where they are?

There is a misconception that many people have around the world, especially developing and third world countries. Many of them do not know or have not been taught to believe and trust God where they are located. Many think that the solution to their financial difficulty lies overseas—not where they are.

In this book, Rich challenges that thought process while he shows the reader how people can prosper anywhere, they are.